# 201
# MUFFINS

# 201
# MUFFINS

· · · · · · · · · · · · · · · · · · · · · · · · · ·

## Moist,
## Mouthwatering
## Morsels

· · · · · · · · · · · · · · · · · · · · · · · · · ·

201 Delicious Recipes
201 Tantalizing Pictures

· · · · · · · · · · · · · · · · · · · · · · · · · ·

## GREGG R. GILLESPIE

**Photographs by Claire Young,
Wild Bill Studios**

BLACK DOG
& LEVENTHAL
PUBLISHERS

Published by
Black Dog & Leventhal Publishers, Inc.
151 West 19th Street
New York, NY  10011

Distributed by
Workman Publishing Company
708 Broadway
New York, NY  10003

Printed and bound in Great Britain by
Butler & Tanner Ltd, Frome & London

Library of Congress Cataloging-in-Publication Data
Gillespie, Gregg R., 1934-
201 muffins : moist, mouthwatering morsels / by
Gregg R. Gillespie.
p. cm.
ISBN 1-57912-116-0
1. Muffins. 2. Bread. I. Title: Two hundred one muffins.
II. Title: Two hundred and one muffins. III. Title.

TX770.M83 G55 2001
641.8'15--dc21

                                                    2001025067

Cover design by Kathy Herlihy-Paoli
Interior design  by Design Duo

j i h g f e d c b a

# TABLE OF CONTENTS

# ALL-SEASON MUFFINS

MAKES: *11 to 12 muffins*

# APPLE-AND-DATE MUFFINS

MAKES: *10 muffins*

2¼ cups all-purpose flour
2½ teaspoons baking powder
1 teaspoon baking soda
2 large eggs
⅓ cup butter or margarine, melted
½ cup granulated sugar
1 teaspoon vanilla extract
1 cup plus 3 tablespoons plain
  yogurt or sour cream

**1** Position the rack in the center of the oven and preheat to 375 degrees F. Lightly grease or line with paper baking cups twelve 2¾-inch muffin cups.

**2** In a large bowl, blend together the flour, baking powder, and baking soda. In a medium bowl, beat the eggs until foamy. Beat in the butter, sugar, vanilla extract, and yogurt. Combine the two mixtures, blending until the dry ingredients are just moistened.

**3** Spoon the batter into the prepared muffin cups, filling each about three-quarters full. Bake for 15 to 20 minutes, or until a cake tester or wooden toothpick inserted into the center of a muffin comes out clean. Cool in the pan on a wire rack for 5 to 7 minutes. Serve warm, or invert onto the rack to cool completely.

1½ cups whole-wheat flour
¾ cup All-Bran® cereal
2 teaspoons baking powder
½ teaspoon ground cinnamon
¼ teaspoon salt
¾ cup peeled, cored, diced apple
¼ cup chopped dates
2 large eggs
¾ cup milk
½ cup warm honey

**1** Position the rack in the center of the oven and preheat to 375 degrees F. Lightly grease or line with paper baking cups twelve 2¾-inch muffin cups.

**2** In a large bowl, blend together the flour, cereal, baking powder, cinnamon, salt, apples, and dates. In a medium bowl, beat the eggs until foamy. Beat in the milk and honey. Combine the two mixtures, blending until the dry ingredients are just moistened.

**3** Spoon the batter into the prepared muffin cups, filling each about three-quarters full. Bake for 15 to 20 minutes, or until a cake tester or wooden toothpick inserted into the center of a muffin comes out clean. Cool in the pan on a wire rack for 5 to 7 minutes. Serve warm, or invert onto the rack to cool completely.

# APPLE-AND-OAT BRAN MUFFINS

MAKES: *11 to 12 muffins*

1¼ cups whole-wheat flour
1 cup oat bran
2½ teaspoons baking powder
¼ teaspoon baking soda
¼ teaspoon ground cinnamon
¾ cup finely chopped apple
¼ teaspoon salt
2 large egg whites
1 cup buttermilk or sour milk
⅓ cup packed light-brown sugar
2 tablespoons canola oil

**1** Position the rack in the center of the oven and preheat to 375 degrees F. Lightly grease or line with paper baking cups twelve 2¾-inch muffin cups.

**2** In a large bowl, blend together the flour, oat bran, baking powder, baking soda, cinnamon, apples, and salt. In a medium bowl, beat the egg whites until foamy. Beat in the buttermilk, sugar, and oil. Combine the two mixtures, blending until the dry ingredients are just moistened.

**3** Spoon the batter into the prepared muffin cups, filling each about three-quarters full. Bake for 15 to 20 minutes, or until a cake tester or wooden toothpick inserted into the center of a muffin comes out clean. Cool in the pan on a wire rack for 5 to 7 minutes. Serve warm, or invert onto the rack to cool completely.

# APPLE-AND-PECAN MUFFINS

MAKES: *12 to 14 muffins*

2½ cups all-purpose flour
1 teaspoon baking soda
1½ cups peeled, cored, and diced apple
½ cup chopped pecans
1 teaspoon salt
1 large egg
1 cup buttermilk or sour milk
1½ cups packed light-brown sugar
¼ cup canola oil
1 teaspoon vanilla extract

**1** Position the rack in the center of the oven and preheat to 375 degrees F. Lightly grease or line with paper baking cups fourteen 2¾-inch muffin cups.

**2** In a large bowl, blend together the flour, baking soda, apples, pecans, and salt. In a medium bowl, beat the egg until foamy. Beat in the buttermilk, brown sugar, oil, and vanilla extract. Combine the two mixtures, blending until the dry ingredients are just moistened.

**3** Spoon the batter into the prepared muffin cups, filling each about three-quarters full. Bake for 20 to 25 minutes, or until a cake tester or wooden toothpick inserted into the center of a muffin comes out clean. Cool in the pan on a wire rack for 5 to 7 minutes. Serve warm, or invert onto the rack to cool completely.

SERVING SUGGESTIONS:
**Serve with apple butter.**

# Applesauce Muffins

Makes: *9 to 10 muffins*

½ cup butter or margarine, at room
   temperature
⅓ cup granulated sugar
2 large eggs
1 cup unsweetened applesauce
1 cup all-purpose flour
¾ cup graham flour
1 tablespoon baking powder
½ cup chopped walnuts
½ teaspoon salt

**1** Position the rack in the center of the oven and preheat to 400 degrees F. Lightly grease or line with paper baking cups ten 2¾-inch muffin cups.

**2** In a large bowl, beat the butter and sugar until light and fluffy. Beat in the eggs, one at a time, beating vigorously after each addition. Stir in the applesauce. In a medium bowl, blend together the two flours, baking powder, walnuts, and salt. Combine the two mixtures, blending until the dry ingredients are just moistened.

**3** Spoon the batter into the prepared muffin cups, filling each about three-quarters full. Bake for 20 to 25 minutes, or until a cake tester or wooden toothpick inserted into the center of a muffin comes out clean. Cool in the pan on a wire rack for 5 to 7 minutes. Serve warm, or invert onto the rack to cool completely.

**Serving suggestion:**
**Serve with apple butter.**

# Apricot-and-Walnut Muffins

Makes: *5 to 6 muffins*

1⅔ cups all-purpose flour
2 teaspoons baking powder
½ cup granulated sugar
¼ teaspoon ground cinnamon
½ teaspoon salt
1 large egg
¾ cup milk
⅓ cup butter or margarine, melted
½ cup apricot jam
½ cup chopped walnuts

**1** Position the rack in the center of the oven and preheat to 400 degrees F. Lightly grease or line with paper baking cups six (makes 5 to 6 muffins) 2¾-inch muffin cups.

**2** In a large bowl, blend together the flour, baking powder, sugar, cinnamon, and salt. In a medium bowl, beat the egg until foamy. Beat in the milk and butter. Combine the two mixtures, blending until the dry ingredients are just moistened.

**3** Spoon the batter into the prepared muffin cups, filling each about three-quarters full. Lightly press 1 teaspoon of apricot jam into the center of each muffin. Sprinkle the top of each muffin with chopped walnuts. Bake for 20 to 25 minutes, or until a wooden toothpick inserted near the edge of a muffin (not into the jam filling) comes out clean. Cool in the pan on a wire rack for 5 to 7 minutes. Serve warm, or invert onto the rack to cool completely.

# AVOCADO MUFFINS

*Makes: 11 to 12 muffins*

2 cups all-purpose flour
2 teaspoons baking powder
¼ cup granulated sugar
½ teaspoon salt
1 cup toasted, slivered almonds
1 large egg
¼ cup butter or margarine, melted
1 cup milk
1 medium ripe avocado, peeled,
    seeded and pureed

**1** Position the rack in the center of the oven and preheat to 375 degrees F. Lightly grease or line with paper baking cups twelve 2¾-inch muffin cups.

**2** In a large bowl, blend together the flour, baking powder, sugar, salt, and almonds. In a small bowl, beat the egg until foamy. Beat in the butter, milk, and pureed avocado. Combine the two mixtures, blending until the dry ingredients are just moistened.

**3** Spoon the batter into the prepared muffin cups, filling each about three-quarters full. Bake for 15 to 20 minutes, or until a cake tester or wooden toothpick inserted into the center of a muffin comes out clean. Cool in the pan on a wire rack for 5 to 7 minutes. Serve warm, or invert onto the rack to cool completely.

# BACON MUFFINS

*Makes: 11 to 12 muffins*

1⅓ cups all-purpose flour
1 tablespoon baking powder
8 slices crisply cooked bacon,
    crumbled
1 teaspoon salt
1 large egg
1 tablespoon granulated sugar
¾ cup milk
1 tablespoon bacon drippings

**1** Position the rack in the center of the oven and preheat to 425 degrees F. Lightly grease or line with paper baking cups twelve 2¾-inch muffin cups.

**2** In a large bowl, blend together the flour, baking powder, crumbled bacon, and salt. In a medium bowl, beat the egg until foamy. Beat in the sugar, milk, and drippings. Combine the two mixtures, blending until the dry ingredients are just moistened.

**3** Spoon the batter into the prepared muffin cups, filling each about three-quarters full. Bake for 15 to 20 minutes, or until a cake tester or wooden toothpick inserted into the center of a muffin comes out clean. Cool in the pan on a wire rack for 5 to 7 minutes. Serve warm, or invert onto the rack to cool completely.

# BANANA-AND-CHOCOLATE-CHIP MUFFINS

MAKES: *9 to 10 muffins*

1¼ cups all-purpose flour
1 tablespoon baking powder
½ cup (3 ounces) semi-sweet chocolate chips
½ teaspoon salt
2 tablespoons packed light-brown sugar
2 tablespoons granulated sugar
⅓ cup butter or margarine, melted
1 large, ripe banana, mashed
1 large egg
¾ cup milk

**1** Position the rack in the center of the oven and preheat to 400 degrees F. Lightly grease or line with paper baking cups ten 2¾-inch muffin cups.

**2** In a large bowl, blend the flour, baking powder, chocolate chips, and salt. In a medium bowl, beat together the sugars, butter, and banana until smooth. Beat in the egg and milk. Combine the two mixtures, blending until the dry ingredients are just moistened.

**3** Spoon the batter into the prepared muffin cups, filling each about three-quarters full. Bake for 15 to 20 minutes, or until a cake tester or wooden toothpick inserted into the center of a muffin comes out clean. Cool in the pan on a wire rack for 5 to 7 minutes. Serve warm, or invert onto the rack to cool completely.

# BANANA CROWNS

MAKES: *11 to 12 muffins*

2 cups all-purpose flour
¾ cup granulated sugar
1 teaspoon baking soda
½ cup chopped walnuts
1 teaspoon salt
2 large eggs
1½ cups (about 3 medium) mashed bananas
2 to 4 tablespoons mango jam or preserves
1 large banana, sliced into 24 pieces

**1** Position the rack in the center of the oven and preheat to 375 degrees F. Lightly grease or line with paper baking cups twelve 2¾-inch muffin cups.

**2** In a large bowl, blend together the flour, sugar, baking soda, walnuts, and salt. In a small bowl, beat the eggs and mashed bananas until smooth. Combine the two mixtures, blending until the dry ingredients are just moistened.

**3** Spoon the batter into the prepared muffin cups, filling each about three-quarters full. Press ¼ teaspoon of the mango jam and a banana slice into the center of each cup. Bake for 15 to 20 minutes, or until a cake tester or wooden toothpick inserted near the edge of a muffin (not into the jam) comes out clean. Cool in the pan on a wire rack for 5 to 7 minutes. Allow to cool to room temperature.

# BANANA–PRALINE MUFFINS

MAKES: *9 to 10 muffins*

1¼ cups all-purpose flour
½ cup plus 2 tablespoons granulated
    sugar
2 teaspoons baking powder
½ teaspoon salt
1 large egg
1 tablespoon sour cream or plain
    yogurt
3 tablespoons packed light-brown
    sugar
⅓ cup chopped pecans
3 large ripe bananas, mashed
⅓ cup canola oil
Coarsely crushed pecans for garnish

**1** Position the rack in the center of the oven and preheat to 400 degrees F. Lightly grease or line with paper baking cups ten 2¾-inch muffin cups.

**2** In a large bowl, blend together the flour, granulated sugar, baking powder, and salt. In a medium bowl, beat the egg foamy. Beat in the sour cream, brown sugar, pecans, bananas, and oil. Combine the two mixes, blending until the dry ingredients are just moistened.

**3** Spoon the batter into the prepared muffin cups, filling each about three-quarters full. Sprinkle pecans over the top of each. Bake for about 12 to 15 minutes, or until a cake tester or wooden toothpick inserted into the center of a muffin comes out clean. Cool in the pan on a wire rack for 5 to 7 minutes. Serve warm, or invert onto the rack to cool completely.

# BANANA–POPPY SEED MUFFINS

MAKES: *11 to 12 muffins*

2 cups all-purpose flour
2 teaspoons baking powder
1½ tablespoons poppy seeds
½ teaspoon salt
1 large egg
¾ cup granulated sugar
¼ cup canola oil
2 teaspoons dried grated orange zest
1 medium ripe banana, mashed

**1** Position the rack in the center of the oven and preheat to 375 degrees F. Lightly grease or line with paper baking cups twelve 2¾-inch muffin cups.

**2** In a large bowl, blend together the flour, baking powder, poppy seeds, and salt. In a medium bowl, beat the egg foamy. Beat in the sugar, oil, orange zest, and banana. Combine the two mixtures, blending until the dry ingredients are just moistened.

**3** Spoon the batter into the prepared muffin cups, filling each about three-quarters full. Bake for 15 to 20 minutes, or until a cake tester or wooden toothpick inserted into the center of a muffin comes out clean. Cool in the pan on a wire rack for 5 to 7 minutes. Serve warm, or invert onto the rack to cool completely.

# BLACKBERRY MUFFINS

MAKES: *5 to 6 muffins*

2½ cups all-purpose flour
1 tablespoon baking powder
½ teaspoon salt
3 large eggs, separated
½ cup granulated sugar
¼ cup canola oil
⅔ cup milk
1 cup blackberries, rinsed and dried

**1** Position the rack in the center of the oven and preheat to 400 degrees F. Lightly grease or line with paper baking cups six 2¼-inch muffin cups.

**2** In a large bowl, blend together the flour, baking powder, and salt. In a medium bowl, beat together the egg yolks, sugar, oil, and milk. In a small bowl, beat the egg whites until stiff but not dry. Fold the blackberries into the egg whites. Combine the dry ingredients and the egg yolk mixture, blending until just moistened. Gently fold in the egg whites.

**3** Spoon the batter into the prepared muffin cups, filling each about three-quarters full. Bake for 20 to 25 minutes, or until a cake tester or wooden toothpick inserted into the center of a muffin comes out clean. Cool in the pan on a wire rack for 5 to 7 minutes. Serve warm, or invert onto the rack to cool completely.

# BLUEBERRY–BANANA MUFFINS

MAKES: *17 to 18 muffins*

2 large eggs
⅓ cup canola oil
½ cup pineapple juice concentrate
1 cup (about 2 medium) mashed ripe bananas
1 tablespoon Triple Sec or concentrated orange juice
2 teaspoons baking soda
¼ teaspoon salt
2 cups all-purpose flour
1 cup fresh blueberries, rinsed and dried

**1** Position the rack in the center of the oven and preheat to 375 degrees F. Lightly grease or line with paper baking cups eighteen 2¼-inch muffin cups.

**2** In a large bowl, beat the eggs until thick and light-colored. Beat in the oil, pineapple juice, bananas, Triple Sec, baking soda, and salt. Stir the flour, blending until the flour is just moistened. Gently fold in the blueberries.

**3** Spoon the batter into the prepared muffin cups, filling each about three-quarters full. Bake for 15 to 20 minutes, or until a cake tester or wooden toothpick inserted into the center of a muffin comes out clean. Cool in the pan on a wire rack for 5 to 7 minutes. Serve warm, or invert onto the rack to cool completely.

# BLUEBERRY–BUTTERMILK MUFFINS

MAKES: *5 to 6 muffins*

2½ cups all-purpose flour
2½ teaspoons baking powder
¼ teaspoon salt
2 large eggs
1 cup granulated sugar
1 cup buttermilk or sour milk
¼ cup butter or margarine, melted
1½ cups blueberries, rinsed and dried

**1** Position the rack in the center of the oven and preheat to 400 degrees F. Lightly grease or line with paper baking cups six 2¾-inch muffin cups.

**2** In a large bowl, blend together the flour, baking powder, and salt. In a medium bowl, beat the eggs until foamy. Beat in the sugar, buttermilk, and melted butter until smooth. Fold in the blueberries. Combine the two mixtures, blending until the dry ingredients are just moistened.

**3** Spoon the batter into the prepared muffin cups, filling each about three-quarters full. Bake for 15 to 20 minutes, or until the tops are golden and a cake tester or wooden toothpick inserted into the center of a muffin comes out clean. Cool in the pan on a wire rack for 5 to 7 minutes. Serve warm, or invert onto the rack to cool completely.

# BLUEBERRY–YOGURT MUFFINS

MAKES: *15 to 16 muffins*

2 cups oat-bran cereal, uncooked
2 teaspoons baking powder
¼ teaspoon salt
2 large egg whites
¼ cup skim milk
2 tablespoons canola oil
¼ cup packed light-brown sugar
¼ cup honey
1 teaspoon grated lemon zest
1 cup (8 ounces) plain yogurt or sour cream
½ cup fresh or frozen blueberries, rinsed and dried

**1** Position the rack in the center of the oven and preheat to 425 degrees F. Lightly grease or line with paper baking cups sixteen 2¾-inch muffin cups.

**2** In a large bowl, blend together the cereal, baking powder, and salt. In a medium bowl, beat the egg whites until stiff but not dry. Stir in the milk, oil, sugar, honey, lemon zest, and yogurt. Fold in the blueberries. Combine the two mixtures, blending until the dry ingredients are just moistened.

**2** Spoon the batter into the prepared muffin cups, filling each about three-quarters full. Bake for 15 to 20 minutes, or until a cake tester or wooden toothpick inserted into the center of a muffin comes out clean. Cool in the pan on a wire rack for 5 to 7 minutes. Serve warm, or invert onto the rack to cool completely.

NOTE: **These muffins are very delicate and will not rise as high as most other muffins**

# Bran Muffins with Raisins

Makes: *11 to 12 muffins*

1¼ cups all-purpose flour
2 cups All-Bran® cereal
2 tablespoons baking powder
1 cup golden raisins
¼ teaspoon salt
1 large egg
1¼ cups milk
½ cup granulated sugar
¼ cup canola oil

**1** Position the rack in the center of the oven and preheat to 400 degrees F. Lightly grease or line with paper baking cups twelve 2¾-inch muffin cups.

**2** In a large bowl, blend together the flour, cereal, baking powder, raisins, and salt. In a medium bowl, beat the egg and milk together until smooth Beat in the sugar and oil. Combine the two mixtures, blending until the dry ingredients are just moistened.

**3** Spoon the batter into the prepared muffin cups, filling each about three-quarters full. Bake for 15 to 20 minutes, or until a cake tester or wooden toothpick inserted into the center of a muffin comes out clean. Cool in the pan on a wire rack for 5 to 7 minutes. Serve warm, or invert onto the rack to cool completely.

# Brown Sugar Muffins

Makes: *11 to 12 muffins*

2 cups all-purpose flour
1 teaspoon baking powder
1 teaspoon baking soda
¼ cup chopped pecans
¼ teaspoon salt
1 large egg
1 cup packed light-brown sugar
½ cup butter or margarine, melted
1 cup milk
2 teaspoons vanilla extract

**1** Position the rack in the center of the oven and preheat to 400 degrees F. Lightly grease or line with paper baking cups twelve 2¾-inch muffin cups.

**2** In a large bowl, blend together the flour, baking powder, baking soda, pecans, and salt. In a medium bowl, beat the egg and brown sugar together until thick. Beat in the butter, milk, and vanilla extract. Combine the two mixtures, blending until the dry ingredients are just moistened.

**3** Spoon the batter into the prepared muffin cups, filling each about three-quarters full. Bake for 15 to 20 minutes, or until a cake tester or wooden toothpick inserted into the center of a muffin comes out clean. Cool in the pan on a wire rack for 5 to 7 minutes. Serve warm, or invert onto the rack to cool completely.

# Butternut Squash Muffins

Makes: *15 to 16 muffins*

# Cajun Corn Muffins

Makes: *11 to 12 muffins*

2 cups all-purpose flour
2 tablespoons granulated sugar
1 tablespoon baking powder
1 teaspoon salt
1 large egg
1 cup milk
¼ cup butter or margarine, melted
⅔ cup cooked butternut squash, mashed

**1** Position the rack in the center of the oven and preheat to 400 degrees F. Lightly grease or line with paper baking cups sixteen 2¾-inch muffin cups.

**2** In a large bowl, blend together the flour, sugar, baking powder, and salt. In a medium bowl, beat the egg, milk, butter, and mashed squash until smooth. Combine the two mixtures, blending until the dry ingredients are just moistened.

**3** Spoon the batter into the prepared muffin cups, filling each about three-quarters full. Bake for 15 to 20 minutes, or until a cake tester or wooden toothpick inserted into the center of a muffin comes out clean. Cool in the pan on a wire rack for 5 to 7 minutes. Serve warm, or invert onto the rack to cool completely.

1½ cups cornmeal
1½ cups all-purpose flour
3 tablespoons granulated sugar
1 tablespoon plus 1½ teaspoons baking powder
1 teaspoon cayenne pepper
1½ teaspoons ground black pepper
½ cup seeded and diced red bell pepper
¼ cup seeded and diced green bell pepper
¼ cup finely minced yellow onion
1½ teaspoons salt
2 large eggs
¼ cup canola oil
1 tablespoon butter or margarine, melted

**1** Position the rack in the center of the oven and preheat to 400 degrees F. Lightly grease or line with paper baking cups twelve 2¾-inch muffin cups.

**2** In a large bowl, blend together the cornmeal, flour, sugar, baking powder, cayenne pepper, black pepper, bell peppers, onions, and salt. In a medium bowl, beat together the eggs, oil, and butter until smooth. Combine the two mixtures, blending until the dry ingredients are just moistened.

**3** Spoon the batter into the prepared muffin cups, filling each about three-quarters full. Bake for 15 to 20 minutes, or until a cake tester or wooden toothpick inserted into the center of a muffin comes out clean. Cool in the pan on a wire rack for 5 to 7 minutes. Serve warm, or invert onto the rack to cool completely.

# Carrot-and-Pineapple Muffins

MAKES: *12 to 14 muffins*

2 cups whole-wheat flour
1 tablespoon baking powder
½ teaspoon ground cinnamon
¼ teaspoon salt
3 medium-size carrots, peeled and grated
One 8¼-ounce can crushed pineapple, drained
1 large egg
1⅓ cups packed dark-brown sugar
¾ cup milk
⅓ cup canola oil
½ teaspoon coconut or almond extract

**1** Position the rack in the center of the oven and preheat to 375 degrees F. Lightly grease or line with paper baking cups fourteen 2¼-inch muffin cups.

**2** In a large bowl, blend together the flour, baking powder, cinnamon, salt, carrots, and pineapple. In a medium bowl, beat together the egg and brown sugar until smooth. Beat in the milk, oil, and coconut extract. Combine the two mixtures, blending until the dry ingredients are just moistened.

**3** Spoon the batter into the prepared muffin cups, filling each about three-quarters full. Bake for 15 to 20 minutes, or until a cake tester or wooden toothpick inserted into the center of a muffin comes out clean. Cool in the pan on a wire rack for 5 to 7 minutes. Serve warm, or invert onto the rack to cool completely.

# Cheddar Cheese-and-Pepper Muffins

MAKES: *11 to 12 muffins*

2 cups all-purpose flour
1 cup (4 ounces) shredded sharp Cheddar cheese
1 tablespoon granulated sugar
1 tablespoon baking powder
1½ teaspoons ground white pepper
½ teaspoon salt
1 large egg
¼ cup canola oil
1¼ cups milk

**1** Position the rack in the center of the oven and preheat to 400 degrees F. Lightly grease or line with paper baking cups twelve 2¼-inch muffin cups.

**2** In a large bowl, blend together the flour, ¾ cup of the cheese, sugar, baking powder, pepper, and salt. In a medium bowl, beat the egg, oil, and milk until smooth. Combine the two mixtures, blending until the dry ingredients are just moistened.

**3** Spoon the batter into the prepared muffin cups, filling each about three-quarters full. Bake for 10 minutes. Sprinkle the remaining ¼ cup of cheese over the tops of the muffins and continue to bake for 5 to 10 minutes more, or until a cake tester or wooden toothpick inserted into the center of a muffin comes out clean. Cool in the pan on a wire rack for 5 to 7 minutes. Serve warm, or invert onto the rack to cool completely.

# Cheesy Bacon-n'-Apple Muffins

Makes: *11 to 12 muffins*

1 medium apple, peeled, cored, and grated
¼ cup granulated sugar
2 cups all-purpose flour
1 tablespoon baking powder
⅔ cup crumbled cooked bacon or bacon bits
¾ cup shredded Cheddar cheese
½ teaspoon salt
1 large egg
1 cup sour milk or butter milk
½ teaspoon baking soda
½ cup butter or margarine, melted

1  Position the rack in the center of the oven and preheat to 375 degrees F. Lightly grease or line with paper baking cups twelve 2¾-inch muffin cups.

2  Place the apple in a small bowl and sprinkle with the sugar. In a large bowl, blend together the flour, baking powder, bacon, cheese, and salt. In a medium bowl, beat the egg until thick and light-colored before beating in the milk, baking soda, and butter. Stir in the apple. Combine the two mixtures, blending until the dry ingredients are just moistened.

3  Spoon the batter into the prepared muffin cups, filling each about three-quarters full. Bake for 15 to 20 minutes, or until a cake tester or wooden toothpick inserted into the center of a muffin comes out clean. Cool in the pan on a wire rack for 5 to 7 minutes. Serve warm, or invert onto the rack to cool completely.

# Cherry Muffins

Makes: *5 to 6 muffins*

2 cups all-purpose flour
1 tablespoon baking powder
1 cup (16 ounces) pitted sweet black cherry halves
¼ teaspoon salt
2 large eggs
⅔ cup granulated sugar
6 tablespoons butter or margarine, melted
½ cup milk
1 teaspoon vanilla extract

1  Position the rack in the center of the oven and preheat to 400 degrees F. Lightly grease or line with paper baking cups six 2¼-inch muffin cups.

2  In a large bowl, blend together the flour, baking powder, cherries, and salt. In a medium bowl, beat the eggs, butter, sugar, milk, and vanilla extract until smooth. Combine the two mixtures, blending until the dry ingredients are just moistened.

3  Spoon the batter into the prepared muffin cups, filling each about three-quarters full. Bake for 15 to 20 minutes, or until a cake tester or wooden toothpick inserted into the center of a muffin comes out clean. Cool in the pan on a wire rack for 5 to 7 minutes. Serve warm, or invert onto the rack to cool completely.

# CHIVE DINNER MUFFINS

*MAKES: 11 to 12 muffins*

2 cups all-purpose flour
2 teaspoons baking powder
¼ teaspoon baking soda
¼ cup snipped fresh chives
1 teaspoon salt
2 tablespoons butter or margarine, melted
1 large egg
⅔ cup sour milk or buttermilk

**1** Position the rack in the center of the oven and preheat to 400 degrees F. Lightly grease or line with paper baking cups twelve 2¾-inch muffin cups.

**2** In a large bowl, blend together the flour, baking powder, baking soda, chives, and salt. In a medium bowl, beat the butter, egg, and milk until smooth. Combine the two mixtures, blending until the dry ingredients are just moistened.

**3** Spoon the batter into the prepared muffin cups, filling each about three-quarters full. Bake for 15 to 20 minutes, or until a cake tester or wooden toothpick inserted into the center of a muffin comes out clean. Cool in the pan on a wire rack for 5 to 7 minutes. Serve warm, or invert onto the rack to cool completely.

# CHOCOLATE CHIP-AND-ORANGE MUFFINS

*MAKES: 11 to 12 muffins*

2 cups all-purpose flour
2 teaspoons baking powder
⅔ cup miniature chocolate chips
2 tablespoons dried grated orange zest
½ teaspoon salt
¾ cup heavy cream
½ cup canola oil
1 large egg
2 teaspoons Triple Sec liqueur
⅓ cup packed dark-brown sugar

**1** Position the rack in the center of the oven and preheat to 400 degrees F. Lightly grease or line with paper baking cups twelve 2¾-inch muffin cups.

**2** In a large bowl, blend together the flour, baking powder, chocolate chips, orange zest, and salt. In a large bowl, beat the cream, oil, egg, Triple Sec, and brown sugar until smooth. Combine the two mixtures, blending until the dry ingredients are just moistened.

**3** Spoon the batter into the prepared muffin cups, filling each about three-quarters full. Bake for 15 to 20 minutes, or until a cake tester or wooden toothpick inserted into the center of a muffin comes out clean. Cool in the pan on a wire rack for 5 to 7 minutes. Serve warm or invert onto the rack to cool completely.

# Chocolate Fudge Muffins

Makes: *23 to 24 muffins*

1 cup butter or margarine
1½ cups granulated sugar
Four 1-ounce squares semi-sweet
   chocolate
2 cups all-purpose flour
½ teaspoon salt
4 large eggs
1 teaspoon vanilla extract

**1** Position the rack in the center of the oven and preheat to 300 degrees F. Lightly grease or line with paper baking cups twenty-four 2¾-inch muffin cups.

**2** In the top of a double boiler set over simmering water, combine the butter and sugar. Cook, stirring occasionally, until smooth. Add the chocolate all at one time and stir constantly until just melted. Remove from the heat.

**3** In a large bowl, blend together the flour and salt. In a medium bowl, beat the eggs until thick and light-colored. Beat in the vanilla extract. Combine the three mixtures, blending until smooth. (The mixture will be very moist.)

**4** Spoon the batter into the prepared muffin cups, filling each about three-quarters full. Bake for 15 to 20 minutes, or until a cake tester or wooden toothpick inserted into the center of a muffin comes out clean. Cool in the pan on a wire rack for 5 to 7 minutes. Serve warm, or invert onto the rack to cool completely.

# Chocolate–Raspberry Muffins

Makes: *12 to 14 muffins*

2 cups all-purpose flour
2 teaspoons baking powder
½ teaspoon baking soda
½ cup granulated sugar
6 ounces semi-sweet chocolate,
   finely chopped
1 large egg
2 tablespoons butter or margarine,
   melted
¾ cup buttermilk or sour milk
1 cup raspberry preserves
finely chopped pecans for sprinkling

**1** Position the rack in the center of the oven and preheat to 375 degrees F. Lightly grease or line with paper baking cups fourteen 2¾-inch muffin cups.

**2** In a large bowl, blend together the flour, baking powder, baking soda, sugar, and chocolate. In a medium bowl, beat the egg, butter, and buttermilk until smooth. Combine the two mixtures, blending until the dry ingredients are just moistened.

**3** Using a rubber spatula, gently fold in the raspberry preserves. Spoon the batter into the prepared muffin cups, filling each about three-quarters full. Sprinkle the top of the muffins with chopped pecans and bake for about 12 to 15 minutes, or until a cake tester or wooden toothpick inserted near the edge of the muffin (not into the preserves) comes out clean. Cool in the pan on a wire rack for 5 to 7 minutes. Serve warm, or invert onto the rack to cool completely.

# CHORIZO–AND–CORN MUFFINS

MAKES: *10 to 12 muffins*

¾ cup chorizo sausage
1¼ cups all-purpose flour
2 teaspoons baking powder
1 teaspoon baking soda
½ teaspoon ground cumin
½ teaspoon ground coriander
1 teaspoon hot Hungarian paprika
1 tablespoon finely chopped
　jalapeño pepper
1 bell pepper, washed, seeded, and
　chopped fine
½ teaspoon garlic powder
½ teaspoon onion powder
2 large eggs
3 tablespoons butter or margarine,
　melted
1 cup buttermilk or sour milk
One 15-ounce can cream-style corn
3 drops Tabasco®

1　Position the rack in the center of the oven and preheat to 375 degrees F. Lightly grease or line with paper baking cups twelve 2¾-inch muffin cups.

2.　Using a sharp knife, remove the meat from the sausage casing and chop into small pieces. Set aside. In a large bowl, blend together the flour, baking powder, baking soda, cumin, coriander, paprika, jalapeño, bell pepper, garlic powder, and onion powder. In a medium bowl, beat the eggs, butter, and buttermilk until smooth. Stir in the corn and Tabasco. Combine the two mixtures, blending until the dry ingredients are just moistened.

3　Spoon the batter into the prepared muffin cups, filling each about three-quarters full. Bake for 15 to 20 minutes, or until a cake tester or wooden toothpick inserted into the center of a muffin comes out clean. Cool in the pan on a wire rack for 5 to 7 minutes. Serve warm, or invert onto the rack to cool completely.

# CINNAMON-AND-RAISIN MUFFINS

MAKES: *9 to 10 muffins*

1½ cups all-purpose flour
2 teaspoons baking powder
1½ teaspoons ground cinnamon
½ cup seedless raisins
¼ teaspoon salt
½ cup packed brown sugar
1 large egg
¼ cup vegetable shortening, melted
½ cup milk

1　Position the rack in the center of the oven and preheat to 375 degrees F. Lightly grease or line with paper baking cups ten 2¾-inch muffin cups.

2　In a large bowl, blend together the flour, baking powder, cinnamon, raisins, and salt. In a medium bowl, beat the sugar, egg, shortening, and milk until smooth. Combine the two mixtures, blending until the dry ingredients are just moistened.

3　Spoon the batter into the prepared muffin cups, filling each about three-quarters full. Bake for 15 to 20 minutes, or until a cake tester or wooden toothpick inserted into the center of a muffin comes out clean. Cool in the pan on a wire rack for 5 to 7 minutes. Serve warm, or invert onto the rack to cool completely.

SERVING SUGGESTION: **Serve with jam or jelly.**

# Citrus Muffins

*Makes: 11 to 12 muffins*

1¾ cups all-purpose flour
1 tablespoon baking powder
3 tablespoons granulated sugar
¼ teaspoon salt
1 tablespoon dried grated orange
   zest
1 tablespoon fresh grated lime zest
1 large egg
¾ cup milk
⅓ cup butter or margarine, melted,
   additional for brushing the
   muffin tops

**1** Position the rack in the center of the oven and preheat to 400 degrees F. Lightly grease or line with paper baking cups twelve 2¾-inch muffin cups.

**2** In a large bowl, blend together the flour, baking powder, sugar, salt, orange zest, and lime zest. In a medium bowl, beat the egg, milk, and butter until smooth. Combine the two mixtures, blending until the dry ingredients are just moistened.

**3** Spoon the batter into the prepared muffin cups, filling each about three-quarters full. Bake for 10 minutes. Remove from the oven and brush the top of the muffins lightly with melted butter. Bake for an additional 5 to 10 minutes, or until a cake tester or wooden toothpick inserted into the center of a muffin comes out clean. Cool in the pan on a wire rack for 5 to 7 minutes. Serve warm or invert onto the rack to cool completely.

# Cocoa–Raisin– Walnut Muffins

*Makes: 14 to 16 muffins*

2¼ cups all-purpose flour
¾ cup granulated sugar
1 tablespoon baking powder
½ cup Dutch-processed cocoa
⅓ cup chopped walnuts
1 cup seedless raisins
½ teaspoon salt
2 large eggs
½ cup butter or margarine, melted
1¼ cups milk

**1** Position the rack in the center of the oven and preheat to 400 degrees F. Lightly grease or line with paper baking cups sixteen 2¾-inch muffin cups.

**2** In a large bowl, blend together the flour, sugar, baking powder, cocoa, walnuts, raisins, and salt. In a medium bowl, beat the eggs, butter, and milk until smooth. Combine the two mixtures, blending until the dry ingredients are just moistened.

**3** Spoon the batter into the prepared muffin cups, filling each about three-quarters full. Bake for 15 to 20 minutes, or until a cake tester or wooden toothpick inserted into the center of a muffin comes out clean. Cool in the pan on a wire rack for 5 to 7 minutes. Serve warm, or invert onto the rack to cool completely.

# Cocoa Spice Muffins

Makes: *23 to 24 muffins*

1¼ cups all-purpose flour
¾ teaspoon baking soda
1 cup granulated sugar
½ cup Dutch-processed cocoa
  powder
½ cup chopped walnuts
½ teaspoon ground cinnamon
¼ teaspoon ground nutmeg
¼ teaspoon ground cloves
¼ teaspoon salt
1 large egg
¾ cup applesauce
¾ cup milk
¼ cup butter or margarine, melted

1  Position the rack in the center of the oven and preheat to 375 degrees F. Lightly grease or line with paper baking cups twenty-four 2¾-inch muffin cups.

2  In a large bowl, blend together the flour, baking soda, sugar, cocoa, walnuts, cinnamon, nutmeg, cloves, and salt. In a medium bowl, beat the egg, applesauce, milk, and butter until smooth. Combine the two mixtures, blending until the dry ingredients are just moistened.

3  Spoon the mixture into the prepared muffin cups, filling each about three-quarters full. Bake for 15 to 20 minutes, or until a cake tester or wooden toothpick inserted into the center of a muffin comes out clean. Cool in the pan on a wire rack for 5 to 7 minutes. Serve warm, or invert onto the rack to cool completely.

# Coconut Muffins

Makes: *11 to 12 muffins*

2 cups all-purpose flour
¼ cup granulated sugar
4 teaspoons baking powder
1 cup flaked coconut
½ teaspoon salt
1 large egg
3 tablespoons butter or margarine,
  melted
1 cup unsweetened coconut milk

1  Position the rack in the center of the oven and preheat to 450 degrees F. Lightly grease or line with paper baking cups twelve 2¾-inch muffin cups.

2  In a large bowl, blend together the flour, sugar, baking powder, coconut, and salt. In a medium bowl, beat the egg, margarine, and coconut milk until smooth. Combine the two mixtures, blending until the dry ingredients are just moistened.

3  Spoon the batter into the prepared muffin cups, filling each about three-quarters full. Bake for 15 to 20 minutes, or until a cake tester or wooden toothpick inserted into the center of a muffin comes out clean. Cool in the pan on a wire rack for 5 to 7 minutes. Serve warm, or invert onto the rack to cool completely.

# COFFEE–GINGER MUFFINS

MAKES: *23 to 24 muffins*

1¾ cups all-purpose flour
½ cup granulated sugar
1 teaspoon baking soda
¼ teaspoon ground ginger
½ teaspoon ground cardamom
¼ teaspoon salt
1 large egg
½ cup molasses
½ cup strong brewed coffee
¼ cup butter or margarine, melted

**1** Position the rack in the center of the oven and preheat to 375 degrees F. Lightly grease or line with paper baking cups twenty-four 2¾-inch muffin cups.

**2** In a large bowl, blend together the flour, sugar, baking soda, ginger, cardamom, and salt. In a medium bowl, beat the egg, molasses, coffee, and butter until smooth. Combine the two mixtures, blending until the dry ingredients are just moistened.

**3** Spoon the batter into the prepared muffin cups, filling each about three-quarters full. Bake for 15 to 20 minutes, or until a cake tester or wooden toothpick inserted into the center of a muffin comes out clean. Cool in the pan on a wire rack for 5 to 7 minutes. Serve warm, or invert onto the rack to cool completely.

# CORN-AND-ZUCCHINI MUFFINS

MAKES: *11 to 12 muffins*

1 cup all-purpose flour
½ cup whole-wheat flour
½ cup graham flour
1 tablespoon baking powder
½ teaspoon salt
1 teaspoon garlic powder
½ cup shredded zucchini
½ cup whole-kernel corn
2 large egg whites
1¼ cups milk
2 tablespoons butter or margarine, melted

**1** Position the rack in the center of the oven and preheat to 375 degrees F. Lightly grease or line with paper baking cups twelve 2¾-inch muffin cups.

**2** In a large bowl, blend together the three flours, baking powder, garlic powder, salt, zucchini, and corn. In a medium bowl, beat the egg whites until stiff but not dry before beating in the milk and butter. Combine the two mixtures, blending until the dry ingredients are just moistened.

**3** Spoon the batter into the prepared muffin cups, filling each about three-quarters full. Bake for 15 to 20 minutes, or until a cake tester or wooden toothpick inserted into the center of a muffin comes out clean. Cool in the pan on a wire rack for 5 to 7 minutes. Serve warm, or invert onto the rack to cool completely.

# CORNFLAKE–PECAN MUFFINS

MAKES: *11 to 12 muffins*

1 cup all-purpose flour
1 tablespoon baking powder
2 tablespoons granulated sugar
½ teaspoon ground allspice
½ cup chopped pecans
1 cup cornflakes
½ teaspoon salt
1 large egg
⅔ cup milk
3 tablespoons butter or margarine, melted

**1** Position the rack in the center of the oven and preheat to 425 degrees F. Lightly grease or line with paper baking cups twelve 2¾-inch muffin cups.

**2** In a large bowl, blend together the flour, baking powder, sugar, allspice, pecans, cornflakes, and salt. In a medium bowl, beat the egg, milk, and butter until smooth. Combine the two mixtures, blending until the dry ingredients are just moistened.

**3** Spoon the batter into the prepared muffin cups, filling each about three-quarters full. Bake for 15 to 20 minutes, or until a cake tester or wooden toothpick inserted into the center of a muffin comes out clean. Cool in the pan on a wire rack for 5 to 7 minutes. Serve warm, or invert onto the rack to cool completely.

# CORNMEAL MUFFINS WITH BERRIES

MAKES: *11 to 12 muffins*

1 cup all-purpose flour
1 cup coarse cornmeal
2 tablespoons granulated sugar
1 teaspoon baking powder
¼ teaspoon salt
1 large egg
1 cup skim milk
1 tablespoon butter or margarine, melted
1 cup fresh blueberries

**1** Position the rack in the center of the oven and preheat to 425 degrees F. Lightly grease or line with paper baking cups twelve 2¾-inch muffin cups.

**2** In a large bowl, blend together the flour, cornmeal, sugar, baking powder, and salt. In a medium bowl, beat the egg, milk, and butter until smooth. Stir in the blueberries. Combine the two mixtures, blending until the dry ingredients are just moistened.

**3** Spoon the mixture into the prepared muffin cups, filling each about three-quarters full. Bake for 15 to 20 minutes, or until a cake tester or wooden toothpick inserted into the center of a muffin comes out clean. Cool in the pan on a wire rack for 5 to 7 minutes. Serve warm, or invert onto the rack to cool completely.

# Country-Time Okra Muffins

MAKES: *12 to 14 muffins*

# Crab Muffins

MAKES: *16 to 18 muffins*

2 cups all-purpose flour
2½ teaspoons baking powder
½ teaspoon baking soda
2 cups thinly sliced fresh okra
½ cup finely chopped onions
½ teaspoon salt
2 large eggs
1 tablespoon brown sugar
½ cup butter or margarine, melted
1¼ cups milk
1 teaspoon steak sauce of choice
¼ teaspoon bottled hot sauce
Grated Swiss cheese for sprinkling

**1** Position the rack in the center of the oven and preheat to 375 degrees F. Lightly grease or line with paper baking cups fourteen 2¾-inch muffin cups.

**2** In a large bowl, blend together the flour, baking powder, baking soda, okra, onions, and salt. In a medium bowl, beat the eggs until thick and light-colored. Beat in the sugar, butter, milk, steak sauce, and hot sauce until smooth. Combine the two mixtures, blending until the dry ingredients are just moistened.

**3** Spoon the batter into the prepared muffin cups, filling each about three-quarters full. Sprinkle cheese over the top of each of the muffins. Bake for 15 to 20 minutes, or until a cake tester or wooden toothpick inserted into the center of a muffin comes out clean. Cool in the pan on a wire rack for 5 to 7 minutes. Serve warm, or invert onto the rack to cool completely.

3 cups all-purpose flour
5 teaspoons baking powder
1 tablespoon granulated sugar
½ cup finely chopped crabmeat
½ teaspoon dry mustard powder
½ teaspoon ground white pepper
1½ cups milk
½ cup brandy
Grated Gruyère cheese for topping

**1** Position the rack in the center of the oven and preheat to 375 degrees F. Lightly grease or line with paper baking cups eighteen 2¾-inch muffin cups.

**2** In a large bowl, blend together the flour, baking powder, sugar, crabmeat, mustard, and pepper. Make a well in the center of the mixture and pour in the milk and brandy. Combine the ingredients, blending until the dry ingredients are just moistened.

**3** Spoon the mixture into the prepared muffin cups, filling each about three-quarters full, and sprinkle a little Gruyère cheese over the top of each muffin. Bake for 15 to 20 minutes, or until a cake tester or wooden toothpick inserted into the center of a muffin comes out clean. Cool in the pan on a wire rack for 5 to 7 minutes. Serve warm, or invert onto the rack to cool completely.

SERVING SUGGESTION: **Serve with a cheese of choice and a dry white wine.**

# CRANBERRY MUFFINS

MAKES: *14 to 16 muffins*

2 cups all-purpose flour
¾ cup granulated sugar
1 tablespoon baking powder
½ teaspoon salt
1 large egg
1 cup milk
¼ cup butter or margarine, melted
1 cup chopped dried cranberries

**1** Position the rack in the center of the oven and preheat to 400 degrees F. Lightly grease or line with paper baking cups sixteen 2¾-inch muffin cups.

**2** In a large bowl, blend together the flour, sugar, baking powder, and salt. In a medium bowl, beat the egg, milk, and butter until smooth. Fold in the cranberries. Combine the two mixtures, blending until the dry ingredients are just moistened.

**3** Spoon the batter into the prepared muffin cups, filling each about three-quarters full. Bake for 15 to 20 minutes, or until a cake tester or wooden toothpick inserted into the center of a muffin comes out clean. Cool in the pan on a wire rack for 5 to 7 minutes. Serve warm, or invert onto the rack to cool completely.

# CRANBERRY–ORANGE MUFFINS WITH WALNUTS

MAKES: *12 to 14 muffins*

1½ cups all-purpose flour
1 cup rolled oats
½ cup granulated sugar
1 tablespoon baking powder
½ cup chopped walnuts or pecans
¼ teaspoon salt
1 large egg
1 cup milk
¼ cup canola oil
1 cup dried cranberries

**1** Position the rack in the center of the oven and preheat to 400 degrees F. Lightly grease or line with paper baking cups fourteen 2¾-inch muffin cups.

**2** In a large bowl, blend together the flour, oats, sugar, baking powder, walnuts, and salt. In a medium bowl, beat the egg, milk, and oil until smooth. Stir in the cranberries. Combine the two mixtures, blending until the dry ingredients are just moistened.

**3** Spoon the batter into the prepared muffin cups, filling each about three-quarters full. Bake for 15 to 20 minutes, or until a cake tester or wooden toothpick inserted into the center of a muffin comes out clean. Cool in the pan on a wire rack for 5 to 7 minutes. Invert onto the rack to cool completely.

# Cranberry-and-Wheat-Berry Muffins

*Makes: 9 to 10 muffins*

1 cup all-purpose flour
1 cup whole-wheat flour
½ cup wheat berries
1 teaspoon baking soda
½ teaspoon salt
½ cup butter or margarine
1 cup packed brown sugar
2 large eggs
¾ cup sour cream
2 cups fresh chopped cranberries

**1** Position the rack in the center of the oven and preheat to 375 degrees F. Lightly grease or line with paper baking cups ten 2¾-inch muffin cups.

**2** In a large bowl, blend together the two flours, wheat berries, baking soda, and salt. In a medium bowl, cream together the butter and sugar before beating in the eggs and sour cream. Fold in the cranberries. Combine the two mixtures, blending until the dry ingredients are just moistened.

**3** Spoon the batter into the prepared muffin cups, filling each about three-quarters full. Bake for 15 to 20 minutes, or until a cake tester or wooden toothpick inserted into the center of a muffin comes out clean. Cool in the pan on a wire rack for 5 to 7 minutes. Serve warm, or invert onto the rack to cool completely.

# Cream Cheese-Filled Muffins with Raspberries

*Makes: 12 muffins*

2 cups all-purpose flour
1 tablespoon baking powder
2 tablespoons granulated sugar
½ teaspoon salt
1 large egg
1 cup milk
¼ cup canola oil
1 package (8 ounces) cream cheese, cut into 12 chunks
28 to 32 raspberries

**1** Position the rack in the center of the oven and preheat to 425 degrees F. Lightly grease or line with paper baking cups twelve 2¾-inch muffin cups.

**2** In a large bowl, blend together the flour, baking powder, sugar, and salt. In a small bowl, beat the egg until foamy. Beat in the milk and oil. Combine the two mixtures, blending until the dry ingredients are just moistened.

**3** Spoon 1 heaping tablespoon of the batter into the prepared muffin cups. Press a cube of cream cheese into the center of each and top with two raspberries. Spoon a second tablespoon of the remaining batter on top of the raspberries. Bake for 15 to 20 minutes, or until a cake tester or wooden toothpick inserted near the edge of a muffin (not into the cream cheese) comes out clean. Cool in the pan on a wire rack for 5 to 7 minutes. Serve warm, or invert onto the rack to cool completely.

# CRUMB MUFFINS WITH RAISINS

MAKES: *9 to 10 muffins*

# CRUNCH-APPLE MUFFINS

MAKES: *5 to 6 muffins*

1 cup dry cracked-wheat bread
   crumbs
½ cup seedless raisins
¾ cup sour milk or buttermilk
½ cup all-purpose flour
2 teaspoons caraway seeds
2 teaspoons baking powder
½ teaspoon salt
1 large egg
½ tablespoon butter or margarine,
   melted

**1** Position the rack in the center
of the oven and preheat to 425
degrees F. Lightly grease or line
with paper baking cups ten 2¼-
inch muffin cups.

**2** In a medium bowl, blend the
bread crumbs, raisins, and sour
milk together. Set aside. In a
large bowl, blend together the
flour, caraway seeds, baking
powder, and salt. In a small
bowl, beat the egg until thick
and light-colored. Beat in the
butter. Fold in the bread-crumbs
mixture. Combine the two mixtures, blending until the dry
ingredients are just moistened.

**3** Spoon the batter into the prepared muffin cups, filling each
about three-quarters full. Bake
for 15 to 20 minutes, or until a
cake tester or wooden toothpick
inserted into the center of a muffin comes out clean. Cool in the
pan on a wire rack for 5 to 7
minutes. Serve warm, or invert
onto the rack to cool completely.

2 cups all-purpose flour
⅓ cup granulated sugar
⅓ cup instant nonfat dry milk
   powder
4 teaspoons baking powder
1 cup (about 2 medium) peeled,
   cored, and finely chopped apples
1 teaspoon ground cinnamon
1 teaspoon salt
1 large egg
¼ cup canola oil
¾ cup water

**1** Position the rack in the center
of the oven and preheat to 400
degrees F. Lightly grease or line
with paper baking cups six 2¼-
inch muffin cups.

**2** In a large bowl, blend together
the flour, sugar, milk powder,
baking powder, apples, cinnamon, and salt. In a medium
bowl, beat the egg, oil, and
water until smooth. Combine the
two mixtures, blending until the
dry ingredients are just
moistened.

3 Spoon the batter into the prepared muffin cups, filling each
about three-quarters full. Bake
for 17 to 22 minutes, or until a
cake tester or wooden toothpick
inserted into the center of a muffin is removed clean. Cool in the
pan on a wire rack for 5 to 7
minutes. Serve warm, or invert
onto the rack to cool completely.

# Dark-and-Moist Bran Muffins

MAKES: *30 to 32 muffins*

1½ cups whole-wheat flour
½ cup all-purpose flour
1½ cups bran flakes
2 tablespoons granulated sugar
1¼ teaspoons baking soda
¼ teaspoon salt
1 large egg
2 cups buttermilk or sour milk
½ cup dark molasses
2 tablespoons butter or margarine, melted

**1** Position the rack in the center of the oven and preheat to 375 degrees F. Lightly grease or line with paper baking cups thirty-two 2¾-inch muffin cups.

**2** In a large bowl, blend together the two flours, bran flakes, sugar, baking soda, and salt. In a medium bowl, beat the egg, buttermilk, molasses, and butter until smooth. Combine the two mixtures, blending until the dry ingredients are just moistened.

**3** Spoon the batter into the prepared muffin cups, filling each about three-quarters full. Bake for 15 to 20 minutes, or until a cake tester or wooden toothpick inserted into the center of a muffin comes out clean. Cool in the pan on a wire rack for 5 to 7 minutes. Serve warm, or invert onto the rack to cool completely.

# Date-and-Nut Muffins

MAKES: *14 to 16 muffins*

2 cups all-purpose flour
¼ cup granulated sugar
4 teaspoons baking powder
½ package (7¼ ounces) pitted dates, chopped
¼ cup chopped walnuts or pecans
½ teaspoon salt
1 large egg
¼ cup butter or margarine, melted
1 cup hot milk

**1** Position the rack in the center of the oven and preheat to 400 degrees F. Lightly grease or line with paper baking cups sixteen 2¾-inch muffin cups.

**2** In a large bowl, blend together the flour, sugar, baking powder, dates, walnuts, and salt. In a medium bowl, beat the egg until thick and light-colored before beating in the butter. Beat in the hot milk a little at a time. Combine the two mixtures, blending until the dry ingredients are just moistened.

**3** Spoon the batter into the prepared muffin cups, filling each about three-quarters full. Bake for 15 to 20 minutes, or until a cake tester or wooden toothpick inserted into the center of a muffin comes out clean. Cool in the pan on a wire rack for 5 to 7 minutes. Serve warm, or invert onto the rack to cool completely.

# Deluxe Orange Muffins

MAKES: *16 to 18 muffins*

2 cups all-purpose flour
1 tablespoon baking powder
¾ teaspoon salt
1 large egg
⅓ cup granulated sugar
¼ cup canola oil
¼ cup Triple Sec
½ cup orange juice
1 tablespoon grated orange zest

**1** Position the rack in the center of the oven and preheat to 400 degrees F. Lightly grease or line with paper baking cups eighteen 2¾-inch muffin cups.

**2** In a large bowl, blend together the flour, baking powder, and salt. In a medium bowl, beat the egg until foamy. Beat in the sugar. Beat in the oil, Triple Sec, juice, and orange zest until smooth. Combine the two mixtures, blending until the dry ingredients are just moistened.

**3** Drop 1 heaping tablespoon of the batter into the prepared muffin cups, filling each about three-quarters full. Bake for 15 to 20 minutes, or until a cake tester or wooden toothpick inserted into the center of a muffin comes out clean. Cool in the pan on a wire rack for 5 to 7 minutes. Serve warm, or invert onto the rack to cool completely.

# Dill-and-Thyme Muffins

MAKES: *12 to 14 muffins*

⅔ cup oat bran
⅔ cup all-purpose flour
⅔ cup whole-wheat flour
1 tablespoon baking powder
1½ teaspoons dried dill, crushed
½ teaspoon dried thyme, crushed
¼ teaspoon garlic powder
1 teaspoon nonfat dry milk powder
½ teaspoon salt
1 cup milk
½ cup cottage cheese or ricotta cheese
¼ cup butter or margarine, melted
2 large egg whites
1 teaspoon canola oil

**1** Position the rack in the center of the oven and preheat to 425 degrees F. Lightly grease or line with paper baking cups fourteen 2¾-inch muffin cups.

**2** In a large bowl, blend together the oat bran, two flours, baking powder, dill, thyme, garlic powder, milk powder, and salt. In a medium bowl, beat the milk, cheese, butter, egg whites, and oil until smooth. Combine the two mixtures, blending until the dry ingredients are just moistened.

**3** Spoon the batter into the prepared muffin cups, filling each about three-quarters full. Bake for 15 to 20 minutes, or until a cake tester or wooden toothpick inserted into the center of a muffin comes out clean. Cool in the pan on a wire rack for 5 to 7 minutes. Serve warm, or invert onto the rack to cool completely.

# Double Chocolate Muffins

Makes: *11 to 12 muffins*

2 cups all-purpose flour
1 tablespoon baking powder
¾ cup Dutch-processed cocoa powder
½ teaspoon salt
1½ cups (7¾ ounces) miniature semi-sweet chocolate chips
½ cup vegetable shortening
1 cup granulated sugar
1 large egg
1 cup warm milk

**1** Position a rack in the center of the oven and preheat to 400 degrees F. Lightly grease or line with paper baking cups twelve 2¾-inch muffin cups.

**2** In a large bowl, blend together the flour, baking powder, cocoa, salt, and chocolate chips. In a medium bowl, beat the shortening and sugar until fluffy. Beat in the egg and milk. Combine the two mixtures, blending until the dry ingredients are just moistened.

**3** Spoon the batter into the prepared muffin cups, filling each about three-quarters full. Bake for 15 to 20 minutes or until a cake tester or wooden toothpick inserted into the center of a muffin comes out clean. Cool in the pan on a wire rack for 5 to 7 minutes. Serve warm, or invert onto the rack to cool completely.

Serving suggestion: **Serve with chocolate ice cream.**

# Dried-Fruit Muffins

Makes: *11 to 12 muffins*

2 cups all-purpose flour
1 tablespoon baking powder
½ cup chopped mixed dried fruits
½ teaspoon salt
2 large eggs
¼ cup packed light-brown sugar
½ cup butter or margarine, melted
¾ cup milk
¼ teaspoon raspberry flavoring

**1** Position the rack in the center of the oven and preheat to 400 degrees F. Lightly grease or line with paper baking cups twelve 2¾-inch muffin cups.

**2** In a large bowl, blend together the flour, baking powder, dried fruits, and salt. In a medium bowl, beat the egg until thick and light-colored. Beat in the brown sugar, butter, milk, and flavoring until smooth. Combine the two mixtures, blending until the dry ingredients are just moistened.

**3** Spoon the batter into the prepared muffin cups, filling each about three-quarters full. Bake for 15 to 20 minutes, or until a cake tester or wooden toothpick inserted into the center of a muffin comes out clean. Cool in the pan on a wire rack for 5 to 7 minutes. Serve warm, or invert onto the rack to cool completely.

# Early-Morning Breakfast Muffins

Makes: *8 to 10 muffins*

1½ cups all-purpose flour
2 teaspoons baking powder
1½ tablespoons packed brown sugar
⅛ teaspoon salt
¾ cup milk
¼ cup butter or margarine, melted
12 slices crisp, cooked bacon, crumbled
4 large eggs
¾ cup shredded Cheddar cheese
Pinch freshly ground black pepper

**1** Position the rack in the center of the over and preheat to 375 degrees F. Lightly grease or line with paper baking cups ten 2¾-inch muffin cups.

**2** In a large bowl, blend together the flour, baking powder, brown sugar, and salt. In a medium bowl, blend the milk and butter together before stirring in the bacon. Combine the two mixtures, blending until the dry ingredients are just moistened.

**3** Drop 1½ heaping tablespoons of the batter into each of the prepared muffin cups. In a medium bowl, beat the eggs until thick and light-colored. Beat in the cheese and pepper. Spoon this mixture evenly over the tops of the muffins in the pan and bake for 15 to 20 minutes, or until a cake tester or wooden toothpick inserted into the center of a muffin comes out clean. Cool in the pan on a wire rack for 5 to 7 minutes.

# Eggless Graham Muffins

Makes: *19 to 20 muffins*

1 cup all-purpose flour
1½ cups graham flour
¾ teaspoon baking powder
1 teaspoon baking soda
¼ cup granulated sugar
½ teaspoon salt
3 tablespoons butter or margarine, melted
1½ cups buttermilk or sour milk

**1** Position the rack in the center of the oven and preheat to 400 degrees F. Lightly grease or line with paper baking cups twenty 2¾-inch muffin cups.

**2** In a large bowl, blend together the two flours, baking powder, baking soda, sugar, and salt. In a medium bowl, blend the butter and buttermilk until smooth. Combine the two mixtures, blending until the dry ingredients are just moistened.

**3** Spoon the batter into the prepared muffin cups, filling each about three-quarters full. Bake for 15 to 20 minutes, or until a cake tester or wooden toothpick inserted into the center of a muffin comes out clean. Cool in the pan on a wire rack for 5 to 7 minutes. Serve warm, or invert onto the rack to cool completely.

# Eggless Rainbow Muffins

**Makes:** *11 to 12 muffins*

2 cups all-purpose flour
4 teaspoons baking powder
2 tablespoons rainbow sprinkles
½ teaspoon salt
¾ cup milk
¼ cup butter or margarine, melted

**1** Position the rack in the center of the oven and preheat to 400 degrees F. Lightly grease or line with paper baking cups twelve 2¾-inch muffin cups.

**2** In a large bowl, blend together the flour, baking powder, sprinkles, and salt. In a small bowl, beat the milk and margarine until smooth. Combine the two mixtures, blending until the dry ingredients are just moistened.

**3** Spoon the batter into the prepared muffin cups, filling each about three-quarters full. Bake for 15 to 20 minutes, or until a cake tester or wooden toothpick inserted into the center of a muffin comes out clean. Cool in the pan on a wire rack for 5 to 7 minutes. Serve warm, or invert onto the rack to cool completely.

# Fig–All-Bran Muffins

**Makes:** *23 to 24 muffins*

¾ cup all-purpose flour
1 tablespoon baking powder
¼ teaspoon baking soda
1 cup dried figs, washed, trimmed, and chopped
2 large eggs
3 tablespoons butter or margarine, melted
2 tablespoons dark molasses
1 cup milk
2¼ cups All-Bran® cereal

**1** Position the rack in the center of the oven and preheat to 425 degrees F. Lightly grease or line with paper baking cups twenty-four 2¾-inch muffin cups.

**2** In a large bowl, blend together the flour, baking powder, baking soda, and figs. In a medium bowl, beat the eggs until thick and light-colored before beating in the butter, molasses, and milk. Stir in the All-Bran. Combine the two mixtures, blending until the dry ingredients are just moistened.

**3** Spoon the batter into the prepared muffin cups, filling each about three-quarters full. Bake for 12 to 15 minutes, or until a cake tester or wooden toothpick inserted into the center of a muffin comes out clean. Cool in the pan on a wire rack for 5 to 7 minutes. Serve warm, or invert onto the rack to cool completely.

# Fresh Fruit, Oat, and Bran Muffins

**Makes:** *23 to 24 muffins*

2 cups whole-wheat flour
1 cup rolled oats
½ cup unprocessed wheat bran
½ cup packed brown sugar
1½ teaspoons baking soda
1½ teaspoons ground cinnamon
1 teaspoon salt
2 large eggs
1½ cups buttermilk
¼ cup canola oil
1 tablespoon orange juice
3 cups finely chopped peaches

**1** Position the rack in the center of the oven and preheat to 400 degrees F. Lightly grease or line with paper baking cups twenty-four 2¾-inch muffin cups.

**2** In a large bowl, blend together the flour, oats, wheat bran, brown sugar, baking soda, cinnamon, and salt. In a medium bowl, beat the eggs until foamy. Beat in the buttermilk, oil, and orange juice. Stir in the chopped peaches. Combine the two mixtures, blending until the dry ingredients are just moistened.

**3** Spoon the batter into the prepared muffin cups, filling each about three-quarters full. Bake for 15 to 20 minutes, or until a cake tester or wooden toothpick inserted into the center of a muffin comes out clean. Cool in the pan on a wire rack for 5 to 7 minutes. Serve warm, or invert onto the rack to cool completely.

# Fresh Peach Muffins

**Makes:** *11 to 12 muffins*

1 cup chopped fresh peaches or fresh apricots
1 teaspoon lemon juice
⅔ cup granulated sugar
2 cups all-purpose flour
1 tablespoon baking powder
½ teaspoon ground cinnamon
1 large egg
1 cup milk
¼ cup butter or margarine, melted

**1** Position the rack in the center of the oven and preheat to 450 degrees F. Lightly grease or line with paper baking cups twelve 2¾-inch muffin cups.

**2** Place the peaches in a small bowl and sprinkle them with lemon juice and 1 tablespoon of the sugar. Set aside. In a large bowl, blend together the flour, remaining sugar, baking powder, and cinnamon. In a medium bowl, beat the egg until thick and light-colored. Beat in the milk and margarine. Stir in the peaches. Combine the two mixtures, blending until the dry ingredients are just moistened.

**3** Spoon the batter into the prepared muffin cups, filling each about three-quarters full. Bake for 15 to 20 minutes, or until a cake tester or wooden toothpick inserted into the center of a muffin comes out clean. Cool in the pan on a wire rack for 5 to 7 minutes. Serve warm, or invert onto the rack to cool completely.

# Fresh Pumpkin– Buttermilk Muffins

Makes: *12 to 14 muffins*

1 cup all-purpose flour
½ cup whole-wheat flour
½ cup granulated sugar
1 teaspoon baking powder
1 teaspoon Cunningham® English Mixture (see Note)
½ cup finely chopped pecans or hazelnuts
½ teaspoon salt
1 large egg
¼ cup butter or margarine, at room temperature
½ cup buttermilk
1 tablespoon Amaretto liqueur or 1 teaspoon almond extract
1 cup grated fresh pumpkin, with rind

**1** Position the rack in the center of the oven and preheat to 400 degrees F. Lightly grease or line with paper baking cups twelve 2¾-inch muffin cups.

**2** In a large bowl, blend together the two flours, sugar, baking powder, spice, nuts, and salt. In a medium bowl, beat the egg until thick and light-colored. Beat in the butter, buttermilk, and Amaretto. Stir in the pumpkin. Combine the two mixtures, blending until the dry ingredients are just moistened.

**3** Spoon the batter into the prepared muffin cups, filling each about three-quarters full. Bake for 15 to 20 minutes, or until a cake tester or wooden toothpick inserted into a muffin comes out clean. Cool in the pan on a wire rack for 5 to 7 minutes. Serve warm, or invert onto the rack to cool completely.

Note: If you can't find the Cunningham® English mixture use ¾ teaspoon cinnamon and ¼ teaspoon nutmeg.

# Fruit-Filled Muffins

Makes: *6 to 8 muffins*

2 cups Bisquick® baking mix
2 tablespoons granulated sugar
⅔ cup skim milk
1 tablespoon canola oil
¼ cup cholesterol-free egg product
1 tablespoon Amaretto liqueur
¼ cup fruit preserves

**1** Position the rack in the center of the oven and preheat to 400 degrees F. Lightly grease or line with paper baking cups eight 2¾-inch muffin cups.

**2** In a large bowl, blend together the Bisquick, and sugar. In a medium bowl, beat the milk, oil, Amaretto, and egg product until smooth. Combine the two mixtures, blending until the dry ingredients are just moistened.

**3** Spoon the batter into the prepared muffin cups, filling each about three-quarters full. Using a small spoon, divide the fruit preserves evenly between the cups into the center of each muffin. Bake for 15 to 20 minutes, or until a cake tester or wooden toothpick inserted at the edge of a muffin (not into the preserves) comes out clean. Cool in the pan on a wire rack for 5 to 7 minutes. Serve warm, or invert onto the rack to cool completely.

# Fruity Buckwheat Muffins

Makes: *11 to 12 muffins*

1 cup all-purpose flour
¾ cup buckwheat flour
1½ teaspoons baking powder
¼ teaspoon baking soda
⅓ cup granulated sugar
1 cup finely diced Granny Smith apples, peeled and cored
¼ cup finely diced dates
¾ cup buttermilk or sour milk
2 tablespoons canola oil
1 large egg

**1** Position the rack in the center of the oven and preheat to 375 degrees F. Lightly grease or line with paper baking cups twelve 2¼-inch muffin cups.

**2** In a large bowl, blend together the two flours, baking powder, baking soda, sugar, apples, and dates. In a medium bowl, beat the buttermilk, oil, and egg until smooth. Combine the two mixtures, blending until the dry ingredients are just moistened.

**3** Spoon the batter into the prepared muffin cups, filling each about three-quarters full. Bake for about 18 to 20 minutes, or until a cake tester or wooden toothpick inserted into the center of a muffin comes out clean. Cool in the pan on a wire rack for 5 to 7 minutes. Serve warm, or invert onto the rack to cool completely.

# Garden Herb Muffins

Makes: *12 to 14 muffins*

2 cups all-purpose flour
2 teaspoons baking powder
1 teaspoon garlic powder
1 teaspoon dry mustard powder
¼ cup chopped fresh scallions (green onions)
¼ cup grated fresh carrots (save the greens)
1 teaspoon dried crushed tarragon
½ teaspoon dried crushed thyme
½ teaspoon dried chervil
¼ teaspoon salt
2 large egg whites
1 cup skim milk
2 tablespoons butter or margarine, melted
2 tablespoons sour cream or plain yogurt
Grated Romano cheese for sprinkling

**1** Position the rack in the center of the oven and preheat to 375 degrees F. Lightly grease or line with paper baking cups fourteen 2¼-inch muffin cups.

**2** In a large bowl, blend together the flour, baking powder, garlic powder, mustard, scallions, carrots, thyme, chervil, and salt. In a medium bowl, beat the egg whites until stiff but not dry. Beat in the milk, butter, and sour cream. Combine the two mixtures, blending until the dry ingredients are just moistened.

**3** Spoon the batter into the prepared muffin cups, filling each about three-quarters full. Sprinkle Romano cheese over the tops of the muffins. Bake for 15 to 20 minutes, or until a cake tester or wooden toothpick inserted into the center of a muffin comes out clean. Cool in the pan on a wire rack for 5 to 7 minutes. Serve warm, or invert onto the rack to cool completely.

# GARLIC-AND-CORN MUFFINS

MAKES: *12 to 14 muffins*

1½ cups all-purpose flour
⅔ cup yellow cornmeal
4 teaspoons granulated sugar
1 tablespoon baking powder
½ teaspoon baking soda
1½ teaspoons garlic powder
1¼ teaspoons salt
2 large eggs
½ cup butter or margarine, melted
1 cup buttermilk or sour milk
1 cup whole-kernel corn

**1** Position the rack in the center of the oven and preheat to 425 degrees F. Lightly grease or line with paper baking cups fourteen 2¾-inch muffin cups.

**2** In a large bowl, blend together the flour, cornmeal, sugar, baking powder, baking soda, garlic powder, and salt. In a medium bowl, beat the eggs until thick and light-colored. Beat in the butter and buttermilk. Stir in the corn. Combine the two mixtures, blending until the dry ingredients are just moistened.

**3** Spoon the batter into the prepared muffin cups, filling each about three-quarters full. Bake for 15 to 20 minutes, or until a cake tester or wooden toothpick inserted into the center of a muffin comes out clean. Cool in the pan on a wire rack for 5 to 7 minutes. Serve warm, or invert onto the rack to cool completely.

# GERMAN MUFFINS

MAKES: *15 to 16 muffins*

¾ cup butter or margarine, at room temperature
½ cup granulated sugar
2 large eggs
4 teaspoons rum
1 teaspoon vanilla extract
3 tablespoons milk
2¼ cups all-purpose flour
2 teaspoons baking powder
½ teaspoon ground cinnamon
¼ teaspoon salt
¼ cup finely ground hazelnuts
1 tablespoon grated orange zest
¼ cup seedless raisins

**1** Position the rack in the center of the oven and preheat to 375 degrees F. Lightly grease or line with paper baking cups sixteen 2¾-inch muffin cups.

**2** In a medium bowl, beat the butter and sugar until light and fluffy before beating in the eggs, rum, vanilla, and milk. In a large bowl, blend together the flour, baking powder, cinnamon, salt, hazelnuts, orange zest, and raisins. Combine the two mixtures, blending until the dry ingredients are just moistened.

**3** Spoon the batter into the prepared muffin cups, filling each about three-quarters full. Bake for 15 to 20 minutes, or until a cake tester or wooden toothpick inserted into the center of a muffin comes out clean. Cool in the pan on a wire rack for 5 to 7 minutes. Serve warm, or invert onto the rack to cool completely.

# Ginger-and-Molasses Muffins

Makes: *29 to 30 muffins*

# Gingerbread Muffins

Makes: *11 to 12 muffins*

3 cups all-purpose flour
½ cup graham flour
1½ teaspoons baking powder
1 teaspoon baking soda
2 teaspoons ground allspice
¼ cup finely chopped fresh, peeled
    ginger root
¼ teaspoon salt
¼ cup finely chopped pecans
1 cup golden raisins (optional)
4 large eggs, separated
1 cup granulated sugar
½ cup butter or margarine, melted
1 cup molasses
1 cup sour milk or buttermilk

**1** Position the rack in the center of the oven and preheat to 375 degrees F. Lightly grease or line with paper baking cups thirty 2¾-inch muffin cups.

**2** In a large bowl, blend together the two flours, baking powder, baking soda, allspice, ginger, salt, pecans, and raisins. In a medium bowl, beat the egg whites until stiff but not dry. Beat in the sugar, butter, molasses, and buttermilk. Combine the two mixtures, blending until the dry ingredients are just moistened.

**3** Spoon the batter into the prepared muffin cups, filling each about three-quarters full. Bake for 15 to 20 minutes, or until a cake tester or wooden toothpick inserted into the center of a muffin comes out clean. Cool in the pan on a wire rack for 5 to 7 minutes. Serve warm, or invert onto the rack to cool completely.

1½ cups all-purpose flour
1 cup oat bran
1 teaspoon baking powder
1 teaspoon baking soda
1 teaspoon ground ginger
½ teaspoon ground cinnamon
⅛ teaspoon ground cardamom
3 tablespoons packed light-brown
    sugar
1 teaspoon nonfat dry milk powder
½ cup golden raisins
½ teaspoon salt
2 large egg whites
¼ cup molasses
¼ cup butter or margarine, melted
¾ cup sour milk or buttermilk
1 teaspoon canola oil
1 teaspoon vanilla extract

**1** Position the rack in the center of the oven and preheat to 400 degrees F. Lightly grease or line with paper baking cups twelve 2¾-inch muffin cups.

**2** In a large bowl, blend together the flour, oat bran, baking powder, baking soda, ginger, cinnamon, cardamom, brown sugar, milk powder, raisins, and salt. In a medium bowl, beat the egg whites until stiff but not dry. Beat in the molasses, butter, milk, oil, and vanilla extract. Combine the two mixtures, blending until the dry ingredients are just moistened.

**3** Spoon the batter into the prepared muffin cups, filling each about three-quarters full. Bake for 15 to 20 minutes, or until a cake tester or wooden toothpick inserted into the center of a muffin comes out clean. Cool in the pan on a wire rack for 5 to 7 minutes. Serve warm, or invert onto the rack to cool completely.

# GRANOLA MUFFINS

MAKES: *11 to 12 muffins*

1 cup all-purpose flour
1¾ cups granola cereal
¼ cup granulated sugar
2½ teaspoons baking powder
½ cup seedless raisins
1 large egg
1 cup milk
¼ cup canola oil

**1** Position the rack in the center of the oven and preheat to 375 degrees F. Lightly grease or line with paper baking cups twelve 2¾-inch muffin cups.

**2** In a large bowl, blend together the flour, cereal, sugar, baking powder, and raisins. In a medium bowl, beat the egg until thick and light-colored. Beat in the milk and oil. Combine the two mixtures, blending until the dry ingredients are just moistened.

**3** Spoon the batter into the prepared muffin cups, filling each about three-quarters full. Bake for 15 to 20 minutes, or until a cake tester or wooden toothpick inserted into the center of a muffin comes out clean. Cool in the pan on a wire rack for 5 to 7 minutes. Serve warm, or invert onto the rack to cool completely.

# GRAPE MUFFINS

MAKES: *11 to 12 muffins*

1 cup whole-wheat flour
1 cup cornmeal
1 tablespoon baking powder
¼ teaspoon salt
¼ teaspoon ground allspice
½ cup finely chopped pecans, plus
    more for topping the muffins
1 large egg
1 tablespoon canola oil
¼ cup grape-flavored yogurt (or
    berry-flavored yogurt)
1¼ cups grape-juice concentrate
1 teaspoon lemon juice

**1** Position the rack in the center of oven and preheat to 375 degrees F. Lightly grease or line with paper baking cups twelve 2¾-inch muffin cups.

**2** In a large bowl, blend together the flour, cornmeal, baking powder, salt, allspice, and pecans. In a medium bowl, beat the egg until foamy. Beat in the oil, yogurt, grape juice, and lemon juice. Combine the two mixtures, blending until the dry ingredients are just moistened.

**3** Spoon the batter into the prepared muffin cups, filling each about three-quarters full. Sprinkle the tops of the muffins lightly with pecans. Bake for 15 to 20 minutes, or until a cake tester or wooden toothpick inserted into the center of a muffin comes out clean. Cool in the pan on a wire rack for 5 to 7 minutes. Serve warm, or invert onto the rack to cool completely.

# Hawaiian Nut Muffins

Makes: *11 to 12 muffins*

2 cups all-purpose flour
2 teaspoons baking powder
½ teaspoon baking soda
½ cup chopped macadamia nuts
½ cup canned pineapple, crushed
  and drained
½ teaspoon salt
2 large eggs
¼ cup packed light-brown sugar
¼ cup butter or margarine, melted
¾ cup milk

**1** Position the rack in the center of the oven and preheat to 400 degrees F. Lightly grease or line with paper baking cups twelve 2¼-inch muffin cups.

**2** In a large bowl, blend together the flour, baking powder, baking soda, nuts, pineapple, and salt. In a medium bowl, beat the eggs until foamy. Beat in the sugar, butter, and milk. Combine the two mixtures, blending until the dry ingredients are just moistened.

**3** Spoon the batter into the prepared muffin cups, filling each about three-quarters full. Bake for 15 to 20 minutes, or until a cake tester or wooden toothpick inserted into the center of a muffin comes out clean. Cool in the pan on a wire rack for 5 to 7 minutes. Serve warm, or invert onto the rack to cool completely.

# Heirloom Raisin Muffins

Makes: *5 to 6 muffins*

1 cup raisins
½ cup warmed brandy
1½ cups all-purpose flour
1 teaspoon baking powder
¼ cup granulated sugar
½ cup butter or margarine, at room
  temperature
2 large eggs, at room temperature

**1** Position the rack in the center of the oven and preheat to 400 degrees F. Lightly grease or line with paper baking cups six 2¼-inch muffin cups.

**2** Place the raisins in a cup or small bowl and pour in the brandy. Set aside for 20 minutes.

**3** Drain the raisins, discarding the brandy or saving it for another use. In a large bowl, blend together the flour, baking powder, and drained raisins. In a small bowl, cream the sugar and butter together. Beat in the eggs, one at a time, beating well after each addition. Combine the two mixtures, blending until the dry ingredients are just moistened.

**4** Spoon the batter into the prepared muffin cups, filling each about three-quarters full. Bake for about 18 to 22 minutes, or until a cake tester or wooden toothpick inserted into the center of a muffin comes out clean. Cool in the pan on a wire rack for 5 to 7 minutes. Serve warm, or invert onto the rack to cool completely.

# HERBAL MUFFINS WITH POLENTA

*MAKES: 18 to 20 muffins*

3 tablespoons olive oil
¼ cup packed light-brown sugar
2 cups coarsely chopped onions
3 cups all-purpose flour
¼ cup baking powder
1 teaspoon crushed cumin seeds
1 teaspoon crushed red-pepper flakes
¼ cup chopped fresh parsley
1 tablespoon chopped fresh tarragon
2 large eggs
6 tablespoons butter or margarine, melted
1⅓ cups milk
2 cups finely chopped pre-cooked polenta

1  Position the rack in the center of the oven and preheat to 375 degrees F. Lightly grease or line with paper baking cups twenty 2¾-inch muffin cups.

2  In a medium skillet set over a medium heat, combine the olive oil and brown sugar. As soon as the sugar has melted, add the chopped onion and cook, stirring frequently, until the onions have turned a dark golden color. Remove from the heat and set aside to cool.

3  In a large bowl, blend together the flour, baking powder, cumin, red-pepper flakes, parsley, and tarragon. In a medium bowl, combine the eggs, butter, and milk and beat until smooth. Stir in the polenta, stirring until combined but still slightly lumpy. Combine the two mixtures with three strokes. Add the onions and continue to stir until the dry ingredients are just moistened and the onions are well incorporated.

4  Spoon the batter into the prepared muffin cups, filling each about three-quarters full. Bake for about 20 to 25 minutes, or until a cake tester or wooden toothpick inserted into the center of a muffin comes out clean. Cool in the pan on a wire rack for 5 to 7 minutes. Serve warm, or invert onto the rack to cool completely.

# High-Fiber Muffins

**Makes:** *11 to 12 muffins*

1 cup all-purpose flour
1 tablespoon baking powder
3 cups canola cereal
½ teaspoon ground cinnamon
Pinch salt
1 large egg
⅓ cup packed light-brown sugar
1 cup milk
⅓ cup canola oil

**1** Position the rack in the center of the oven and preheat to 400 degrees F. Lightly grease or line with paper baking cups twelve 2¾-inch muffin cups.

**2** In a large bowl, blend together the flour, baking powder, cereal, cinnamon, and salt. In a medium bowl, beat the egg until foamy. Beat in the brown sugar, milk, and oil. Combine the two mixtures, blending until the dry ingredients are just moistened.

**3** Spoon the batter into the prepared muffin cups, filling each about three-quarters full. Bake for 15 to 20 minutes, or until a cake tester or wooden toothpick inserted into the center of a muffin comes out clean. Cool in the pan on a wire rack for 5 to 7 minutes. Serve warm, or invert onto the rack to cool completely.

# High-Protein Muffins

**Makes:** *9 to 10 muffins*

1½ cups seedless raisins
½ cup warmed brandy
1 cup soy flour
1 cup whole-wheat flour
4 teaspoons baking powder
1 cup toasted wheat germ
1 teaspoon ground nutmeg
½ teaspoon ground cinnamon
¼ teaspoon salt
2½ cups 40% Bran Flakes®
1¼ cups milk
⅔ cup honey
¼ cup dark molasses
4 large eggs
⅔ cup canola oil

**1** Position the rack in the center of the oven and preheat to 375 degrees F. Lightly grease or line with paper baking cups ten 2¾-inch muffin cups.

**2** Place the raisins in a small bowl and add the warmed brandy. Set aside for 20 minutes.

**3** In a large bowl, blend together the two flours, baking powder, wheat germ, nutmeg, cinnamon, salt, and cereal. In a medium bowl, beat the milk, honey, molasses, eggs, and oil until smooth. Combine the two mixes until the dry ingredients are just moistened. Drain the raisins, discarding the brandy or saving it for another use. Fold the drained raisins into the batter.

**4** Spoon the batter into the prepared muffin cups, filling each about three-quarters full. Sprinkle with the topping and bake for 20 to 25 minutes, or until a cake tester or wooden toothpick inserted into the center of a muffin comes out clean. Remove from oven and cool in the pan on a wire rack for 5 to 7 minutes. Serve warm, or invert onto the rack to cool completely.

# HONEY-CURRANT MUFFINS

MAKES: *11 to 12 muffins*

1¾ cups all-purpose flour
¼ cup graham flour
1 tablespoon baking powder
½ cup currants
1 teaspoon salt
1 large egg
1 cup milk
¼ cup honey
2 tablespoons Amaretto liqueur
¼ cup butter or margarine, melted

**1** Position the rack in the center of the oven and preheat to 400 degrees F. Lightly grease or line with paper baking cups twelve 2¾-inch muffin cups.

**2** In a large bowl, blend together the two flours, baking powder, currants, and salt. In a medium bowl, beat the egg, milk, honey, Amaretto, and butter until smooth. Combine the two mixtures, blending until the dry ingredients are just moistened.

**3** Spoon the batter into the prepared muffin cups, filling each about three-quarters full. Bake for 15 to 20 minutes, or until a cake tester or wooden toothpick inserted into the center of a muffin comes out clean. Cool in the pan on a wire rack for 5 to 7 minutes. Serve warm, or invert onto the rack to cool completely.

# HONEY–OATMEAL MUFFINS WITH FRUIT

MAKES: *5 to 6 muffins*

1 cup all-purpose flour
1½ cups rolled oats
⅓ cup packed brown sugar
1 tablespoon baking powder
1 cup chopped mixed dried fruit
½ teaspoon salt
1 large egg
¼ cup canola oil
½ cup milk
¼ cup honey

**1** Position the rack in the center of the oven and preheat to 400 degrees F. Lightly grease or line with paper baking cups six 2¾-inch muffin cups.

**2** In a large bowl, blend together the flour, oats, brown sugar, baking powder, mixed fruit, and salt. In a medium bowl, beat the egg, oil, milk, and honey until smooth. Combine the two mixtures, blending until the dry ingredients are just moistened.

**3** Spoon the batter into the prepared muffin cups, filling each about three-quarters full. Bake for 15 to 20 minutes, or until a cake tester or wooden toothpick inserted into the center of a muffin comes out clean. Cool in the pan on a wire rack for 5 to 7 minutes. Serve warm, or invert onto the rack to cool completely.

# Honey–Graham Muffins

Makes: *15 to 17 muffins*

1 cup graham flour
1 cup corn flour
2 teaspoons baking powder
2 tablespoons granulated sugar
1 teaspoon salt
2 large eggs
1 cup milk
¼ cup honey
1 tablespoon butter or margarine,
   melted

**1** Position the rack in the center of the oven and preheat to 425 degrees F. Lightly grease or line with paper baking cups seventeen 2¾-inch muffin cups.

**2** In a large bowl, blend together the two flours, baking powder, sugar, and salt. In a medium bowl, beat the eggs until foamy. Beat in the milk, honey, and butter. Combine the two mixtures, blending until the dry ingredients are just moistened.

**3** Spoon the batter into the prepared muffin cups, filling each about three-quarters full. Bake for 15 to 20 minutes, or until a cake tester or wooden toothpick inserted into the center of a muffin comes out clean. Cool in the pan on a wire rack for 5 to 7 minutes. Serve warm, or invert onto the rack to cool completely.

# Irish Coffee Muffins

Makes: *11 to 12 muffins*

2 cups all-purpose flour
1 tablespoon baking powder
½ teaspoon salt
1 large egg
½ cup granulated sugar
⅓ cup butter or margarine, melted
½ cup heavy cream
¼ cup Irish whiskey
½ cup coffee-flavored liqueur

**1** Position the rack in the center of the oven and preheat to 400 degrees F. Lightly grease or line with paper baking cups twelve 2¾-inch muffin cups.

**2** In a large bowl, blend together the flour, baking powder, and salt. In a medium bowl, beat the egg, sugar, butter, cream, whiskey, and liqueur until smooth. Combine the two mixtures, blending until the dry ingredients are just moistened.

**3** Spoon the batter into the prepared muffin cups, filling each about three-quarters full. Bake for 15 to 20 minutes, or until a cake tester or wooden toothpick inserted into the center of a muffin comes out clean. Cool in the pan on a wire rack for 5 to 7 minutes. Serve warm, or invert onto the rack to cool completely.

# Lemon-and-Poppy-Seed Muffins

Makes: *11 to 12 muffins*

1¾ cups all-purpose flour
⅓ cup plus 2 tablespoons granulated sugar
2 teaspoons baking powder
2 tablespoons grated lemon zest
¼ teaspoon salt
1 large egg
3 tablespoons canola oil
1 tablespoon plus 2 teaspoons poppy seeds
1 cup milk
1 tablespoon lemon juice

**1** Position the rack in the center of the oven and preheat to 400 degrees F. Lightly grease or line with paper baking cups twelve 2¼-inch muffin cups.

**2** In a large bowl, blend together the flour, ⅓ cup of the sugar, the baking powder, lemon zest, and salt. In a medium bowl, beat together the remaining 2 tablespoons of sugar, the egg, oil, 1 tablespoon of the poppy seeds, the milk, and lemon juice. Combine the two mixtures, blending until the dry ingredients are just moistened.

**3** Spoon the batter into the prepared muffin cups, filling each about three-quarters full. Sprinkle the remaining 2 teaspoons of poppy seeds over the tops of the muffins. Bake for 15 to 20 minutes, or until a cake tester or wooden toothpick inserted into the center of a muffin comes out clean. Cool in the pan on a wire rack for 5 to 7 minutes. Serve warm, or invert onto the rack to cool completely.

**Serving suggestion:** Serve with a vanilla custard or tapioca pudding.

# Lime-Flavored Muffins

Makes: *11 to 12 muffins*

2 cups all-purpose flour
2 teaspoons baking powder
½ teaspoon salt
1 large egg
¾ cup evaporated milk
½ cup canola oil
⅓ cup packed light-brown sugar
¼ cup lime-juice concentrate
2 tablespoons freshly grated lime zest
⅔ cup miniature chocolate chips (optional)

**1** Position the rack in the center of the oven and preheat to 400 degrees F. Lightly grease or line with paper baking cups twelve 2¼ muffin cups.

**2** In a large bowl, blend together the flour, baking powder, and salt. In a medium bowl, beat the egg until foamy. Beat in the milk, oil, sugar, lime juice, and lime zest. Combine the two mixtures, blending until the dry ingredients are just moistened. Stir in the optional chocolate chips.

**3** Spoon the batter into the prepared muffin cups, filling each about three-quarters full. Bake for 15 to 20 minutes, or until a cake tester or wooden toothpick inserted into the center of a muffin comes out clean. Cool in the pan on a wire rack for 5 to 7 minutes. Serve warm, or invert onto the rack to cool completely.

# Louisiana Hot Corn Muffins

Makes: *11 to 12 muffins*

1½ cups corn flour
½ cup all-purpose flour
4 teaspoons baking powder
1 teaspoon salt
2 large eggs
2 cups milk
1 tablespoon butter or margarine, melted
2 tablespoons finely chopped jalapeño peppers

**1** Position the rack in the center of the oven and preheat to 425 degrees F. Lightly grease or line with paper baking cups twelve 2¾-inch muffin cups.

**2** In a large bowl, blend together the two flours, baking powder, and salt. In a medium bowl, beat the eggs until foamy. Beat in the milk and butter. Stir in the jalapeño. Combine the two mixtures, blending until the dry ingredients are just moistened.

**3** Spoon the batter into the prepared muffin cups, filling each about three-quarters full. Bake for 15 to 20 minutes, or until a cake tester or wooden toothpick inserted into the center of a muffin comes out clean. Cool in the pan on a wire rack for 5 to 7 minutes. Serve warm, or invert onto the rack to cool completely.

# Mango Muffins

Makes: *11 to 12 muffins*

1 cup rice flour
½ cup millet flour
½ cup oat flour
1 teaspoon baking powder
¼ teaspoon salt
1 large mango, peeled, seeded and chopped fine
¼ cup finely chopped almonds
1 large egg
½ cup honey
3 tablespoons butter or margarine, melted
2 tablespoons coconut flavoring

**1** Position the rack in the center of the oven and preheat to 375 degrees F. Lightly grease or line with paper baking cups twelve 2¾-inch muffin cups.

**2** In a large bowl, combine the three flours, baking powder, salt, mango, and almonds. In a medium bowl, beat the egg, honey, butter, and coconut flavoring until smooth. Combine the two mixtures, blending until the dry ingredients are just moistened.

**3** Spoon the batter into the prepared muffin cups, filling each about three-quarters full. Bake for 15 to 20 minutes, or until a cake tester or wooden toothpick inserted into the center of a muffin comes out clean. Cool in the pan on a wire rack for 5 to 7 minutes. Serve warm, or invert onto the rack to cool completely.

# Maple–Bran Muffins

Makes: *5 to 6 muffins*

1½ cups whole-wheat flour
¾ cup wheat bran
1 tablespoon baking powder
⅓ cup chopped walnuts
½ teaspoon salt
1 large egg
½ cup milk
¼ cup canola oil
½ cup maple syrup

**1** Position the rack in the center of the oven and preheat to 400 degrees F. Lightly grease or line with paper baking cups six 2¼-inch muffin cups.

**2** In a large bowl, blend together the flour, bran, baking powder, walnuts, and salt. In a medium bowl, beat the egg, milk, oil, and maple syrup until smooth. Combine the two mixtures, blending until the dry ingredients are just moistened.

**3** Spoon the batter into the prepared muffin cups, filling each about three-quarters full. Bake for 15 to 20 minutes, or until a cake tester or wooden toothpick inserted into the center of a muffin comes out clean. Cool in the pan on a wire rack for 5 to 7 minutes. Serve warm, or transfer to the rack to cool completely.

# Maple–Pecan Muffins

Makes: *3 to 4 muffins*

1½ cups whole-wheat flour
1½ teaspoons baking powder
½ cup finely chopped pecans
¼ teaspoon salt
¼ cup maple syrup
2 tablespoons butter or margarine, melted
1 large egg
⅔ cup water
1 teaspoon vanilla extract

**1** Position the rack in the center of the oven and preheat to 375 degrees F. Lightly grease or line with paper baking cups four 2¼-inch muffin cups.

**2** In a large bowl, blend together the flour, baking powder, pecans, and salt. In a medium bowl, beat the syrup, butter, egg, water, and vanilla extract until smooth. Combine the two mixtures, blending until the dry ingredients are just moistened.

**3** Spoon the batter into the prepared muffin cups, filling each about three-quarters full. Bake for 15 to 20 minutes, or until a cake tester or wooden toothpick inserted into the center of a muffin comes out clean. Cool in the pan on a wire rack for 5 to 7 minutes. Serve warm, or invert onto the rack to cool completely.

# Marmalade–Almond Muffins

Makes: *11 to 12 muffins*

2 cups all-purpose flour
3 tablespoons baking powder
⅔ cup granulated sugar
2 tablespoons grated orange zest
1 cup ground almonds
2 large eggs
¼ cup butter or margarine, melted
½ cup milk
⅔ cup orange marmalade
¼ cup slivered almonds

**1** Position the rack in the center of the oven and preheat to 375 degrees F. Lightly grease or line with paper baking cups twelve 2¾-inch muffin cups.

**2** In a large bowl, blend together the flour, baking powder, sugar, orange zest, and ground almonds. In a medium bowl, beat the eggs until foamy. Beat in the butter and milk. Stir in the marmalade. Combine the two mixtures, blending until the dry ingredients are just moistened.

**3** Spoon the batter into the prepared muffin cups, filling each about three-quarters full. Sprinkle the slivered almonds over the tops of the muffins. Bake for 15 to 20 minutes, or until a cake tester or wooden toothpick inserted into the center of a muffin comes out clean. Cool in the pan on a wire rack for 5 to 7 minutes. Serve warm, or invert onto the rack to cool completely.

**Serving suggestion: Serve with fresh fruit salad.**

# Mincemeat Muffins

Makes: *11 to 12 muffins*

2 cups all-purpose flour
2 teaspoons baking powder
⅓ cup granulated sugar
¼ teaspoon freshly grated nutmeg
1 teaspoon grated orange zest
1 cup chopped pecans
2 large eggs
⅓ cup milk
1¼ cups prepared mincemeat
6 thin slices orange, halved

**1** Position the rack in the center of the oven and preheat to 400 degrees F. Lightly grease or line with paper baking cups twelve 2¾-inch muffin cups.

**2** In a large bowl, blend together the flour, baking powder, sugar, nutmeg, orange zest, and pecans. In a medium bowl, beat the eggs until foamy. Beat in the milk. Stir in the mincemeat. Combine the two mixtures, blending until the dry ingredients are just moistened.

**3** Spoon the batter into the prepared muffin cups, filling each about three-quarters full. Press a half slice of orange into each of the muffins. Bake for 15 to 20 minutes, or until a cake tester or wooden toothpick inserted near the edge of a muffin (not into the orange slice) comes out clean. Cool in the pan on a wire rack for 5 to 7 minutes. Serve warm, or invert onto the rack to cool completely.

# Mini Muffins

Makes: *35 to 36 muffins*

1 cup all-purpose flour
1¼ cups wheat germ
1¼ cups quick-cooking oats
½ cup packed light-brown sugar
1 tablespoon baking powder
1 teaspoon baking soda
¼ teaspoon salt
¾ cup unsweetened applesauce
½ cup canola oil
1 large egg
1 teaspoon almond extract

**1** Position the rack in the center of the oven and preheat to 400 degrees F. Lightly grease or line with paper baking cups thirty-six 2¾-inch muffin cups.

**2** In a large bowl, blend together the flour, wheat germ, oats, sugar, baking powder, baking soda, and salt. In a medium bowl, beat the applesauce, oil, egg, and almonds extract until smooth. Combine the two mixtures, blending until the dry ingredients are just moistened.

**3** Spoon the batter into each of the prepared muffin cups, filling each about three-quarters full. Bake for 12 to 15 minutes, or until a cake tester or wooden toothpick inserted into the center of a muffin comes out clean. Cool in the pan on a wire rack for 5 to 7 minutes. Serve warm, or invert onto the rack to cool completely.

# Molasses, Raisin, and Bran Muffins

Makes: *11 to 12 muffins*

½ cup seedless raisins
¼ cup boiling water
1½ cups bran cereal
1 cup all-purpose flour
1½ teaspoons baking soda
¼ teaspoon salt
1 large egg
½ cup unsweetened apple juice
¼ cup dark molasses
¼ cup apple-flavored yogurt
¼ cup canola oil

**1** Position the rack in the center of the oven and preheat to 400 degrees F. Lightly grease or line with paper baking cups twelve 2¾-inch muffin cups.

**2** Place the raisins in a cup or small bowl and add the boiling water. Set aside for 20 minutes.

**3** In a large bowl, blend together the cereal, flour, baking soda, and salt. In a medium bowl, beat the egg, apple juice, molasses, yogurt, and oil until smooth. Combine the two mixtures, blending until the dry ingredients are just moistened. Drain the raisins, discarding the liquid, and fold the raisins into the batter.

**4** Spoon the batter into the prepared muffin cups, filling each about three-quarters full. Bake for 15 to 20 minutes, or until a cake tester or wooden toothpick inserted into the center of a muffin comes out clean. Cool in the pan on a wire rack for 5 to 7 minutes. Serve warm, or invert onto the rack to cool completely.

# Mushroom Muffins

Makes: *11 to 12 muffins*

2 cups all-purpose flour
1 tablespoon baking powder
One 4-ounce can chopped
    mushrooms, drained and liquid
    reserved
1 teaspoon salt
1 large egg
¾ cup milk
¼ cup granulated sugar
¼ cup butter or margarine, melted
½ cup grated cheese

**1** Position the rack in the center of the oven and preheat to 400 degrees F. Lightly grease or line with paper baking cups twelve 2¼-inch muffin cups.

**2** In a large bowl, blend together the flour, baking powder, mushrooms, and salt. In a medium bowl, beat the egg until thick and light-colored. Beat in the reserved liquid from the mushrooms, the milk, sugar, and butter. Stir in the cheese. Combine the two mixtures, blending until the dry ingredients are just moistened.

**3** Spoon the batter into the prepared muffin cups, filling each about three-quarters full. Bake for 15 to 20 minutes, or until a cake tester or wooden toothpick inserted into the center of a muffin comes out clean. Cool in the pan on a wire rack for 5 to 7 minutes. Serve warm, or invert onto the rack to cool completely.

# Nut–Bran Muffins

Makes: *5 to 6 muffins*

1 teaspoon ground cinnamon
¼ cup plus 1 teaspoon granulated
    sugar
1 cup all-purpose flour
1 cup bran flakes
1 tablespoon baking powder
½ cup finely chopped walnuts or
    pecans
¼ cup chopped pitted dates
½ teaspoon salt
1 large egg
¼ cup milk
⅓ cup melted butter or margarine

**1** Position the rack in the center of the oven and preheat to 400 degrees F. Lightly grease or line with paper baking cups six 2¼-inch muffin cups.

**2** In a cup, combine the cinnamon and 1 teaspoon of the sugar and set aside. In a large bowl, blend together the flour, bran flakes, baking powder, the remaining quarter cup of sugar, the walnuts, dates, and salt. In a medium bowl, beat the egg until foamy. Beat in the milk and butter. Combine the two mixtures, blending until the dry ingredients are just moistened.

**3** Spoon the batter into the prepared muffin cups, filling each about three-quarters full. Sprinkle the tops of the muffins with the cinnamon-and-sugar. Bake for 15 to 20 minutes, or until a cake tester or wooden toothpick inserted into the center of a muffin comes out clean. Cool in the pan on a wire rack for 5 to 7 minutes. Serve warm, or invert onto the rack to cool completely.

# Nutmeg Muffins

Makes: *16 to 18 muffins*

3 cups all-purpose flour
1½ cups packed brown sugar
¾ cup chilled butter or margarine, cut into chunks
2 teaspoons baking powder
½ teaspoon baking soda
2 teaspoons ground nutmeg
½ teaspoon salt
2 large eggs
1½ cups buttermilk or sour milk

**1**  Position the rack in the center of the oven and preheat to 375 degrees F. Lightly grease or line with paper baking cups eighteen 2¾-inch muffin cups.

**2**  In a large bowl, blend together 2 cups of the flour and the brown sugar. Using a pastry cutter or two knives scissor-fashion, cut the butter into the mixture until it resembles coarse meal. Measure out three-quarter cup of this mixture and set it aside for topping the muffins.

**3**  To the mixture remaining in the bowl, stir in the remaining 1 cup of flour, the baking powder, baking soda, nutmeg, and salt. In a medium bowl, beat the eggs and buttermilk until smooth.

Combine the two mixtures, blending until the dry ingredients are just moistened.

**4**  Spoon the batter into the prepared muffin cups, filling each about three-quarters full. Sprinkle the reserved flour-and-brown sugar mixture over the tops of the muffins. Bake for 15 to 20 minutes, or until a cake tester or wooden toothpick inserted into the center of a muffin comes out clean. Cool in the pan on a wire rack for 5 to 7 minutes. Serve warm, or invert onto the rack to cool completely.

# Oat-and-Jam Muffins

Makes: *11 to 12 muffins*

1 cup rolled oats
1 cup sour milk or buttermilk
½ cup packed dark-brown sugar
1 cup all-purpose flour
2 teaspoons baking powder
1 teaspoon baking soda
1 teaspoon nutmeg or mace
½ teaspoon salt
1 large egg
½ cup butter or margarine, melted
2 tablespoons jam or preserves, warmed

**1** Position the rack in the center of the oven and preheat to 375 degrees F. Lightly grease or line with paper baking cups twelve 2¼-inch muffin cups.

**2** In a small bowl, blend together the oats, buttermilk, and brown sugar. Set aside for 5 to 7 minutes. In a large bowl, blend together the flour, baking powder, baking soda, nutmeg, and salt. In a medium bowl, beat the egg until foamy. Beat in the butter. Fold in the oat mixture. Combine the two mixtures, blending until the dry ingredients are just moistened.

**3** Spoon the batter into the prepared muffin cups, filling each about three-quarters full. Bake for 15 to 20 minutes, or until a cake tester or wooden toothpick inserted into the center of a muffin comes out clean. Remove from the oven and brush the warm jam over the tops of the muffins. Cool in the pan on a wire rack for 5 to 7 minutes. Serve warm, or invert onto the rack to cool completely.

# Oat-Bran Muffins with Almonds

Makes: *12 to 14 muffins*

2¼ cups oat-bran cereal
¼ cup ground almonds
¼ cup golden raisins
2 teaspoons baking powder
¼ teaspoon salt
4 large egg whites
⅓ cup honey
2 tablespoons canola oil
¾ cup milk

**1** Position the rack in the center of the oven and preheat to 425 degrees F. Lightly grease or line with paper baking cups fourteen 2¼-inch muffin cups.

**2** In a large bowl, blend together the cereal, almonds, raisins, baking powder, and salt. In a medium bowl, beat the egg whites, honey, oil, and milk until smooth. Combine the two mixtures, blending until the dry ingredients are just moistened.

**3** Spoon the batter into the prepared muffin cups, filling each about three-quarters full. Bake for 15 to 20 minutes, or until a cake tester or wooden toothpick inserted into the center of a muffin comes out clean. Cool in the pan on a wire rack for 5 to 7 minutes. Serve warm, or invert onto the rack to cool completely.

# Oatmeal Muffins

Makes: *5 to 6 muffins*

1 cup quick-cooking oats
1 cup sour milk or buttermilk
1 cup all-purpose flour
1 teaspoon baking powder
½ teaspoon baking soda
½ cup packed light-brown sugar
½ teaspoon salt
1 large egg
½ cup canola oil

**1** Position the rack in the center of the oven and preheat to 375 degrees F. Lightly grease or line with paper baking cups six 2¾-inch muffin cups.

**2** In a small bowl, combine the oats and milk. Set aside for 1 hour.

**3** In a large bowl, blend together the flour, baking powder, baking soda, sugar, and salt. In a medium bowl, beat the egg and oil until smooth. Stir in the oats and milk. Combine the two mixtures, blending until the dry ingredients are just moistened.

**4** Spoon the batter into the prepared muffin cups, filling each about three-quarters full. Bake for 15 to 20 minutes, or until a cake tester or wooden toothpick inserted into the center of a muffin comes out clean. Cool in the pan on a wire rack for 5 to 7 minutes. Serve warm, or invert onto the rack to cool completely.

# Old-Fashioned German Muffins

Makes: *9 to 11 muffins*

2¼ cups all-purpose flour
2 teaspoons baking powder
¼ cup ground hazelnuts or almonds
1 tablespoon grated orange zest
½ teaspoon ground mace or nutmeg
¼ teaspoon salt
¾ cup butter or margarine, at room temperature
½ cup granulated sugar
2 large eggs
3 tablespoons milk
1 tablespoon rum or brandy
1 teaspoon almond extract
2 tablespoons raspberry preserves

**1** Position the rack in the center of the oven and preheat to 375 degrees F. Lightly grease or line with paper baking cups eleven 2¾-inch muffin cups.

**2** In a large bowl, blend together the flour, baking powder, hazelnuts, orange zest, and mace. In a medium bowl, beat the butter and sugar until light and fluffy. Beat in the eggs, milk, rum, and almond extract until smooth. Combine the two mixtures, blending until the dry ingredients are just moistened.

**3** Spoon the batter into the prepared muffin cups, filling each about three-quarters full. Press ½ teaspoon of the raspberry preserves into the center of each muffin. Bake for 15 to 20 minutes, or until a cake tester or wooden toothpick inserted at the edge of a muffin (not into the preserves) comes out clean. Cool in the pan on a wire rack for 5 to 7 minutes. Serve warm, or invert onto the rack to cool completely.

# Olive-and-Cheese Muffins

Makes: *11 to 12 muffins*

2 cups all-purpose flour
1 tablespoon baking powder
1 cup chopped black olives
1 teaspoon salt
1 large egg
1 cup milk
¼ cup granulated sugar
¼ cup butter or margarine, melted
½ cup grated cheese

**1** Position the rack in the center of the oven and preheat to 400 degrees F. Lightly grease or line with paper baking cups twelve 2¾-inch muffin cups.

**2** In a large bowl, blend together the flour, baking powder, olives, and salt. In a medium bowl, beat the egg until thick and light-colored. Beat in the milk, sugar, and butter. Stir in the cheese. Combine the two mixtures, blending until the dry ingredients are just moistened.

**3** Spoon the batter into the prepared muffin cups, filling each about three-quarters full. Bake for 15 to 20 minutes, or until a cake tester or wooden toothpick inserted into the center of a muffin comes out clean. Cool the pan on a wire rack for 5 to 7 minutes. Serve warm, or invert onto the rack to cool completely.

# Orange–Cranberry Muffins

Makes: *12 to 14 muffins*

## TOPPING
¼ cup packed brown sugar
½ teaspoon ground cinnamon
⅓ cup chopped walnuts

## MUFFIN
2 cups all-purpose flour
¼ cup granulated sugar
1 tablespoon baking powder
½ teaspoon baking soda
½ teaspoon salt
1 large egg
1 cup orange juice
1 teaspoon grated orange zest
¼ cup canola oil
1 cup chopped cranberries

**1** Position the rack in the center of the oven and preheat to 375 degrees F. Lightly grease or line with paper baking cups fourteen 2¾-inch muffin cups.

**2** To make the topping, in a small-size bowl, blend together the brown sugar, cinnamon, and walnuts. Set aside.

**3** In a large bowl, blend together the flour, granulated sugar, baking powder, baking soda, and salt. In a medium bowl, beat the egg, orange juice, orange zest, and oil until smooth. Stir in the cranberries. Combine the two mixtures, blending until the dry ingredients are just moistened.

**4** Spoon the batter into the prepared muffin cups, filling each about three-quarters full. Sprinkle top of muffins with sugar, cinnamon and walnut mixture. Bake for 15 to 20 minutes, or until a cake tester or wooden toothpick inserted into the center of a muffin comes out clean. Cool in the pan on a wire rack for 5 to 7 minutes. Serve warm, or invert onto the rack to cool completely.

# Papaya Muffins

Makes: *11 to 12 muffins*

1 cup dried papaya, finely diced
¼ cup peach-flavored brandy
1¼ cups all-purpose flour
1 cup whole-wheat flour
½ cup granulated sugar
1 tablespoon baking powder
1 teaspoon baking soda
4 large egg whites
1 cup plain yogurt
2 tablespoons butter or margarine, melted

**1** Position the rack in the center of the oven and preheat to 375 degrees F. Lightly grease or line with paper baking cups twelve 2⅜-inch muffin cups.

**2** In a cup or small bowl, combine the papaya and brandy. Set aside for 1 hour.

**3** In a large bowl, blend together the two flours, sugar, baking powder, and baking soda. In a medium bowl, beat the egg whites until stiff but not dry. Beat in the yogurt and butter. Stir in the papaya and brandy. Combine the two mixtures, until the dry ingredients are just moistened.

**4** Spoon the batter into the prepared muffin cups, filling each about three-quarters full. Bake for 15 to 20 minutes, or until a cake tester or wooden toothpick inserted into the center of a muffin comes out clean. Cool in the pan on a wire rack for 5 to 7 minutes. Serve warm, or invert onto the rack to cool completely.

# Parmesan Muffins

Makes: *11 to 12 muffins*

2 cups all-purpose flour
1½ teaspoons baking powder
½ teaspoon baking soda
½ cup grated Parmesan cheese
½ cup chopped fresh parsley
½ teaspoon dried crushed marjoram
¼ cup butter or margarine, melted
1 tablespoon granulated sugar
1¼ cups buttermilk or sour milk
1 large egg

**1** Position the rack in the center of the oven and preheat to 400 degrees F. Lightly grease or line with paper baking cups twelve 2⅜-inch muffin cups.

**2** In large bowl, blend together the flour, baking powder, baking soda, parsley, cheese, and marjoram. In a medium bowl, beat the butter, sugar, buttermilk, and egg until smooth. Combine the two mixtures, blending until the dry ingredients are just moistened.

**3** Spoon the batter into the prepared muffin cups, filling each about three-quarters full. Bake for 15 to 20 minutes, or until a cake tester or wooden toothpick inserted into the center of a muffin comes out clean. Cool in the pan on a wire rack for 5 to 7 minutes. Serve warm, or invert onto the rack to cool completely.

# Passover Muffins

Makes: *7 to 8 muffins*

1 to 2 tablespoons schmaltz
1½ cups matzoh farfel
1 to 1½ cups boiling water
4 large eggs
¼ teaspoon ground white pepper
¼ teaspoon salt

1  Position the rack in the center of the oven and preheat to 400 degrees F. Place a small piece of schmaltz in the bottom of each of eight 2¾-inch muffin cups. Place the muffin cups in the oven while preparing the batter.

2  Place the farfel into a fine-mesh strainer and place the strainer in a large bowl in which the strainer touches the bottom. Gently pour the boiling water over the farfel and let set for 5 minutes or until soggy. Remove the strainer from the bowl, and drain completely. Transfer the farfel to a medium bowl. Using a fork, whip in the eggs, one at a time, beating thoroughly after each addition. Stir in salt and pepper.

3  Remove the muffin cups from the oven and pour out the schmaltz. Spoon the batter into the muffin cups, filling each about three-quarters full. Bake for 25 to 30 minutes, or until a cake tester or wooden toothpick inserted into the center of a muffin comes out clean. Cool in the pan on a wire rack for 5 to 7 minutes. Serve warm, or invert onto the rack to cool completely.

BAKING NOTE: The muffins will rise during baking, but will fall as they start to cool.

# Pine Nut, Pecan, and Sunflower Seed Muffins

Makes: *10 to 12 muffins*

1½ cups all-purpose flour
½ cup granulated sugar
2 tablespoons baking powder
¼ cup toasted pine nuts
¼ cup chopped pecans
¼ cup shelled sunflower seeds
1 large egg
½ cup milk
¼ cup butter or margarine, melted

1  Position the rack in the center of the oven and preheat to 400 degrees F. Lightly grease or line with paper baking cups twelve 2¾-inch muffin cups.

2  In a large bowl, blend together the flour, sugar, baking powder, pine nuts, pecans, and sunflower seeds. In a medium bowl, beat the eggs until foamy. Beat in the milk and butter. Combine the two mixtures, blending until the dry ingredients are just moistened.

3  Spoon the batter into the prepared muffin cups, filling each about three-quarters full. Bake for 15 to 20 minutes, or until a cake tester or wooden toothpick inserted into the center of a muffin comes out clean. Cool in the pan on a wire rack for 5 to 7 minutes. Serve warm, or invert onto the rack to cool completely.

# PINEAPPLE–BACON MUFFINS

MAKES: *11 to 12 muffins*

# PLAIN MUFFINS

MAKES: *12 to 14 muffins*

1 cup all-purpose flour
1 cup cornmeal
1 teaspoon baking powder
¾ teaspoon baking soda
2 large eggs
2 tablespoons brown sugar
1½ cups sour milk or buttermilk
¼ cup bacon drippings
4 strips crisply cooked bacon, crumbled
¾ cup crushed pineapple, drained and mashed

**1** Position the rack in the center of the oven and preheat to 425 degrees F. Lightly grease or line with paper baking cups twelve 2¾-inch muffin cups.

**2** In a large bowl, blend together the flour, cornmeal, baking powder, and baking soda. In a medium bowl, beat the eggs until thick and light-colored. Beat in the sugar, milk, and bacon drippings. Stir in the bacon and pineapple. Combine the two mixtures, blending until the dry ingredients are just moistened.

**3** Spoon the batter into the prepared muffin cups, filling each about three-quarters full. Bake for 15 to 20 minutes, or until a cake tester or wooden toothpick inserted into the center of a muffin comes out clean. Cool in the pan on a wire rack for 5 to 7 minutes. Serve warm, or invert onto the rack to cool completely.

3 cups all-purpose flour
1 tablespoon granulated sugar
4 teaspoons baking powder
½ teaspoon salt
2 large eggs
⅔ cup milk
2 tablespoons butter or margarine, melted

**1** Position the rack in the center of the oven and preheat to 425 degrees F. Lightly grease or line with paper baking cups fourteen 2¾-inch muffin cups.

**2** In a large bowl, blend together the flour, sugar, baking powder, and salt. In a medium bowl, beat the eggs until foamy. Beat in the milk and butter. Combine the two mixtures, blending until the dry ingredients are just moistened.

**3** Spoon the batter into the prepared muffin cups, filling each about three-quarters full. Bake for 15 to 20 minutes, or until a cake tester or wooden toothpick inserted into the center of a muffin comes out clean. Cool in the pan on a wire rack for 5 to 7 minutes. Serve warm, or invert onto the rack to cool completely.

# Poppy Seed Muffins

Makes: *14 to 16 muffins*

2 cups all-purpose flour
¾ cup granulated sugar
1 tablespoon baking powder
½ teaspoon grated orange zest
¼ teaspoon ground nutmeg
¼ cup chopped pecans
2 tablespoons poppy seeds
½ cup seedless raisins (optional)
½ teaspoon salt
2 large eggs
1 cup butter or margarine, melted
1 cup milk

**1** Position the rack in the center of the oven and preheat to 400 degrees F. Lightly grease or line with paper baking cups sixteen 2¾-inch muffin cups.

**2** In a large bowl, blend together the flour, sugar, baking powder, orange zest, nutmeg, nuts, poppy seeds, raisins, and salt. In a medium bowl, beat the eggs until foamy. Beat in the butter and milk. Combine the two mixtures, blending until the dry ingredients are just moistened.

**3** Spoon the batter into the prepared muffin cups, filling each about three-quarters full. Bake for 15 to 20 minutes, or until a cake tester or wooden toothpick inserted into the center of a muffin comes out clean. Cool in the pan on a wire rack for 5 to 7 minutes. Serve warm, or invert onto the rack to cool completely.

**Serving suggestion: Serve with black currant jam.**

# Potato Muffins

Makes: *11 to 12 muffins*

2 cups all-purpose flour
3 tablespoons granulated sugar
1 tablespoon baking powder
1 teaspoon ground sage
½ teaspoon onion powder
½ teaspoon salt
1 large egg
¼ cup butter or margarine, melted
1 cup milk
1 cup mashed potatoes
Shredded Swiss cheese for topping

**1** Position the rack in the center of the oven and preheat to 375 degrees F. Lightly grease or line with paper baking cups twelve 2¾-inch muffin cups.

**2** In a large bowl, blend together the flour, sugar, baking powder, sage, onion powder, and salt. In a medium bowl, beat the egg until foamy. Beat in the butter, milk, and mashed potatoes. Combine the two mixtures, blending until the dry ingredients are just moistened.

**3** Spoon the batter into the prepared muffin cups, filling each about three-quarters full. Sprinkle the top of the muffins lightly with the shredded cheese. Bake for 15 to 20 minutes, or until a cake tester or wooden toothpick inserted into the center of a muffin comes out clean. Cool in the pan on a wire rack for 5 to 7 minutes. Serve warm, or invert onto the rack to cool completely.

# PRUNE MUFFINS

*Makes: 8 to 10 muffins*

1 cup all-purpose flour
½ cup graham flour
2 teaspoons baking powder
½ teaspoon baking soda
½ cup dried prunes, chopped
½ teaspoon salt
1 large egg
½ cup sour milk or buttermilk
½ cup warm honey
¼ cup butter or margarine, melted

**1**  Position the rack in the center of the oven and preheat to 375 degrees F. Lightly grease or line with paper baking cups ten 2¼-inch muffin cups.

**2**  In a large bowl, blend together the two flours, baking powder, baking soda, prunes, and salt. In a medium bowl, beat the egg until thick and light-colored. Beat in the milk, honey, and butter. Combine the two mixtures, blending until the dry ingredients are just moistened.

**3**  Spoon the batter into the prepared muffin cups, filling each about three-quarters full. Bake for 15 to 20 minutes, or until a cake tester or wooden toothpick inserted into the center of a muffin comes out clean. Cool in the pan on a wire rack for 5 to 7 minutes. Serve warm, or invert onto the rack to cool completely.

# PUMPKIN MUFFINS

*Makes: 11 to 12 muffins*

1¼ cups all-purpose flour
1½ teaspoons baking powder
1 teaspoon baking soda
¼ teaspoon salt
1 large egg
¼ cup packed light-brown sugar
½ cup butter or margarine, melted
¼ cup molasses
1 cup cooked fresh or canned
   pumpkin pulp

**1**  Position the rack in the center of the oven and preheat to 375 degrees F. Lightly grease or line with paper baking cups twelve 2¼-inch muffin cups.

**2**  In a large bowl, blend together the flour, baking powder, baking soda, and salt. In a medium bowl, beat the egg until foamy. Beat in the brown sugar, butter, and molasses until smooth. Stir in the pumpkin. Combine the two mixtures, blending until the dry ingredients are just moistened.

**3**  Spoon the batter into the prepared baking cups, filling each about three-quarters full. Bake for 15 to 20 minutes, or until a cake tester or wooden toothpick inserted into the center of a muffin comes out clean. Cool in the pan on a wire rack for 5 to 7 minutes. Serve warm, or invert onto the rack to cool completely.

# Rhubarb-Filled Muffins

Makes: *12 to 14 muffins*

1½ cups fresh rhubarb, chopped
¼ cup granulated sugar
¼ teaspoon grated lemon zest
1 tablespoon fresh lemon juice
1 tablespoon water
2½ cups all-purpose flour
2 tablespoons baking powder
1 large egg
3 tablespoons butter or
    margarine, melted
1 cup milk

**1** Position the rack in the center of the oven and preheat to 400 degrees F. Lightly grease or line with paper baking cups fourteen 2¾-inch muffin cups.

**2** In a small bowl, combine the rhubarb, sugar, lemon zest, lemon juice, and water. Blend thoroughly. Set glaze aside.

**3** In a medium bowl, blend the flour and baking powder together. In another medium bowl, beat the egg until thick and light-colored. Beat in the butter and milk. Combine the two mixtures, blending until the dry ingredients are just moistened.

**4** Spoon the batter into the prepared muffin cups, filling each about three-quarters full. Press a tablespoonful of the rhubarb filling into the center of each muffin. Bake for 15 to 20 minutes, or until a cake tester or wooden toothpick inserted into the edge of a muffin (not into the filling) comes out clean. Remove from the oven and immediately brush with the glaze. Cool in the pan on a wire rack for 5 to 7 minutes. Serve warm, or invert onto to the rack to cool completely.

# RICE MUFFINS

MAKES: *11 to 12 muffins*

1½ cups all-purpose flour
¼ cup granulated sugar
2 teaspoons baking powder
½ teaspoon salt
1 large egg
3 tablespoons butter or margarine, melted
1 cup milk
1½ teaspoons almond extract
1 cup cold cooked flavored rice (such as Jasmine or Basmati)

**1** Position the rack in the center of the oven and preheat to 425 degrees F. Lightly grease or line with paper baking cups twelve 2¾-inch muffin cups.

**2** In a large bowl, blend together the flour, sugar, baking powder, and salt. In a medium bowl, beat the egg, butter, milk, and almond extract until smooth. Stir in the rice. Combine the two mixtures, blending until the dry ingredients are just moistened.

**3** Spoon the batter into the prepared muffin cups, filling each about three-quarters full. Bake for 15 to 20 minutes, or until a cake tester or wooden toothpick inserted into the center of a muffin comes out clean. Cool in the pan on a wire rack for 5 to 7 minutes. Serve warm, or invert onto the rack to cool completely.

# RICE-AND-CORNMEAL MUFFINS

MAKES: *12 to 14 muffins*

1¼ cups cooked Jasmine rice (or Basmati)
1 cup white cornmeal
2 tablespoons granulated sugar
2 large eggs, separated
½ teaspoon plus 1/8 teaspoon salt
2 tablespoons butter or margarine, at room temperature
2 teaspoons baking powder
¾ cup plus 1 tablespoon milk

**1** Position the rack in the center of the oven and preheat to 400 degrees F. Lightly grease or line with paper baking cups fourteen 2¾-inch muffin cups.

**2** In a large bowl, using a fork or wire whisk, blend together the rice, cornmeal, and sugar. In a small bowl, beat the egg whites and 1/8 teaspoon salt until the whites are stiff but not dry. In a medium bowl, beat the remaining 1/2 teaspoon salt, butter, baking powder, and milk until smooth. Stir the milk mixture into the rice and cornmeal mixture, blending until the dry ingredients are just moistened. Fold in the egg whites.

**3** Spoon the batter into the prepared muffin cups, filling each about three-quarters full. Bake for 15 to 20 minutes, or until a cake tester or wooden toothpick inserted into the center of a muffin comes out clean. Cool in the pan on a wire rack for 5 to 7 minutes. Serve warm, or invert onto the rack to cool completely.

SERVING SUGGESTION: **Serve with cured Swiss cheese and a dry red wine.**

# Ricotta Cheese Muffins

Makes: *12 to 14 muffins*

1 cup all-purpose flour
½ cup whole-wheat flour
2 teaspoons baking powder
½ teaspoon baking soda
¼ cup Dutch-processed cocoa powder
¼ teaspoon salt
3 large eggs
½ cup butter or margarine, melted
¼ cup honey
½ cup milk
1 cup ricotta or cream cheese
¼ cup coarsely ground walnuts

**1** Position the rack in the center of the oven and preheat to 375 degrees F. Lightly grease or line with paper baking cups fourteen 2¾-inch muffin cups.

**2** In a large bowl, blend together the two flours, baking powder, baking soda, cocoa powder, and salt. In a medium bowl, beat the eggs, butter, honey, milk, and ricotta cheese until smooth. Combine the two mixtures, blending until the dry ingredients are just moistened.

**3** Spoon the batter into the prepared muffin cups, filling each about three-quarters full. Sprinkle the ground nuts over the top of the muffins. Bake for 15 to 20 minutes, or until a cake tester or wooden toothpick inserted into the center of a muffin comes out clean. Cool in the pan on a wire rack for 5 to 7 minutes. Serve warm, or invert onto the rack to cool completely.

# Rye Muffins with Sausage

Makes: *12 to 14 muffins*

1¼ cups rye flour
¾ cup all-purpose flour
2 teaspoons baking powder
¾ teaspoon baking soda
1 tablespoon caraway seeds
½ teaspoon salt
1 large egg
1½ cups sour milk or buttermilk
3 tablespoons molasses
12 to 14 small cocktail sausages

**1** Position the rack in the center of the oven and preheat to 400 degrees F. Lightly grease or line with paper baking cups fourteen 2¾-inch muffin cups.

**2** In a large bowl, blend together the two flours, baking powder, caraway seeds, and salt. In a medium bowl, beat the egg until foamy. Beat in the milk and molasses. Combine the two mixtures, blending until the dry ingredients are just moistened.

**3** Spoon the batter into the prepared muffin cups, filling each about three-quarters full. Press a sausage into the center of each muffin. Bake for 15 to 20 minutes, or until a cake tester or wooden toothpick inserted near the edge of a muffin (not into the sausage) comes out clean. Cool in the pan on a wire rack for 5 to 7 minutes. Serve warm, or invert onto the rack to cool completely.

# Salsa-Bean Muffins

Makes: *18 to 20 muffins*

1⅔ cups all-purpose flour
½ cup corn flour
½ cup cornmeal
1 tablespoon baking powder
1 large egg
3 tablespoons granulated sugar
1½ cups milk
One 19-ounce can (2½ cups)
    Campbell's® Salsa Bean soup

**1** Position the rack in the center
of the oven and preheat to 425
degrees F. Lightly grease or line
with paper baking cups twenty
2¾-inch muffin cups.

**2** In a large bowl, blend together
the two flours, cornmeal, and
baking powder. In a medium
bowl, beat the egg until foamy.
Beat in the sugar, milk, and
soup. Combine the two
mixtures, blending until the dry
ingredients are just moistened.

**3** Spoon the batter into the
prepared muffin cups, filling
each about three-quarters full.
Bake for 15 to 20 minutes, or
until a cake tester or wooden
toothpick inserted into the center
of a muffin comes out clean. Cool
in the pan on a wire rack for 5 to
7 minutes. Serve warm, or invert
onto the rack to cool completely.

# Savory Muffins

Makes: *11 to 12 muffins*

2 cups all-purpose flour
4 teaspoons baking powder
½ teaspoon dried rosemary, crushed
½ teaspoon dried fennel seeds,
    crushed
½ teaspoon dried tarragon
½ teaspoon dried chopped chives
⅓ teaspoon salt
1 large egg
1 cup milk
2 tablespoons butter or margarine,
    melted
1 cup cooked ham or
    chicken, minced

**1** Position the rack in the center
of the oven and preheat to 400
degrees F. Lightly grease or line
with paper baking cups twelve
2¾-inch muffin cups.

**2** In a large bowl, blend together
the flour, baking powder,
rosemary, fennel seeds, tarragon,
chives, and salt. In a medium
bowl, beat the egg until thick
and light-colored. Beat in the
milk and butter. Stir in the
chopped ham. Combine the two
mixtures, blending until the dry
ingredients are just moistened.

**3** Spoon the batter into the
prepared muffin cups, filling
each about three-quarters full.
Bake for 15 to 20 minutes, or
until a cake tester or wooden
toothpick inserted into the
center of a muffin comes out
clean. Cool in the pan on a wire
rack for 5 to 7 minutes. Serve
warm, or invert onto the rack to
cool completely.

# SOUR CREAM MUFFINS

MAKES: *23 to 24 muffins*

1¼ cups all-purpose flour
2 tablespoons granulated sugar
1 teaspoon baking powder
½ teaspoon baking soda
½ teaspoon ground nutmeg
  or mace
½ teaspoon salt
1 large egg
1 cup sour cream

**1** Position the rack in the center of the oven and preheat to 400 degrees F. Lightly grease or line with paper baking cups twenty-four 2¾-inch muffin cups.

**2** In a large bowl, blend together the flour, sugar, baking powder, baking soda, nutmeg, and salt. In a medium bowl, beat the egg foamy. Beat in the sour cream. Combine the two mixtures, blending until the dry ingredients are just moistened.

**3** Spoon the batter into the prepared muffin cups, filling each about three-quarters full. Press ½ teaspoon of the custard into the center of each muffin. Bake for 12 to 18 minutes, or until a cake tester or wooden toothpick inserted into the center of a muffin comes out clean. Cool in the pan on a wire rack for 5 to 7 minutes. Serve warm, or invert onto the rack to cool completely.

# SOUTHEAST ASIA MUFFINS

MAKES: *16 to 18 muffins*

1½ cups rice flour
¾ cup soy flour
2 cups flaked unsweetened coconut, plus more for sprinkling on the muffins
1 tablespoon baking powder
¼ teaspoon five-star spice powder
¼ teaspoon salt
2 large eggs
¼ teaspoon honey
1 cup milk
½ cup canola oil

**1** Position the rack in the center of the oven and preheat to 375 degrees F. Lightly grease or line with paper baking cups eighteen 2¾-inch muffin cups.

**2** In a large bowl, blend together the two flours, coconut, baking powder, spice powder, and salt. In a medium bowl, beat the egg until foamy. Beat in the honey, milk, and oil. Combine the two mixtures, blending until the dry ingredients are just moistened.

**3** Spoon the batter into the prepared muffin cups, filling each about three-quarters full. Sprinkle a little flaked coconut over the top of each muffin. Bake for 15 to 20 minutes, or until a cake tester or wooden toothpick inserted into the center of a muffin comes out clean. Cool in the pan on a wire rack for 5 to 7 minutes. Serve warm, or invert onto the rack to cool completely.

# Soy Muffins

**Makes:** *11 to 12 muffins*

1⅔ cups all-purpose flour
½ cup soy flour
3 tablespoons granulated sugar
1 tablespoon baking powder
1½ teaspoons salt
1 large egg
1¼ cups milk
2 tablespoons butter or
    margarine, melted

**1** Position the rack in the center of the oven and preheat to 425 degrees F. Lightly grease or line with paper baking cups twelve 2¾-inch muffin cups.

**2** In a large bowl, blend together the two flours, sugar, baking powder, and salt. In a medium bowl, beat the egg until foamy. Beat in the milk and butter. Combine the two mixtures, blending until the dry ingredients are just moistened.

**3** Spoon the batter into the prepared muffin cups, filling each about half full. Bake for 15 to 20 minutes, or until a cake tester or wooden toothpick inserted into the center of a muffin comes out clean. Cool in the pan on a wire rack for 5 to 7 minutes. Serve warm, or invert onto the rack to cool completely.

# SPICED SWEET-POTATO MUFFINS

MAKES: *11 to 12 muffins*

¾ cup white corn flour
⅔ cup all-purpose flour
½ cup granulated sugar
2 tablespoons baking powder
1 teaspoon baking soda
1½ teaspoons pumpkin-pie spice
½ cup seedless raisins
½ cup chopped pecans
½ teaspoon salt
2 large eggs
2 tablespoons butter or margarine,
 at room temperature
⅔ cup sour milk or buttermilk
1 tablespoon coffee-flavored liqueur
 or strong brewed coffee
1 teaspoon almond extract
2 cups peeled sweet potatoes, mashed

**1** Position the rack in the center of the oven and preheat to 400 degrees F. Lightly grease or line with paper baking cups twelve 2¼-inch muffin cups.

**2** In a large bowl, blend together the two flours, sugar, baking powder, baking soda, pumpkin-pie spice, raisins, pecans, and salt. In a medium bowl, beat the eggs until thick and light-colored. Beat in the butter, milk, liqueur, almond extract, and potatoes. Combine the two mixtures, blending until the dry ingredients are just moistened.

**3** Spoon the batter into the prepared muffin cups, filling each about three-quarters full. Bake for 15 to 20 minutes, or until a cake tester or wooden toothpick inserted into the center of a muffin comes out clean. Cool in the pan on a wire rack for 5 to 7 minutes. Serve warm, or invert onto the rack to cool completely.

# Spicy Muffins with Cream Cheese

*Makes: 11 to 12 muffins*

2 cups all-purpose flour
½ cup granulated sugar
1 teaspoon baking powder
1 teaspoon ground nutmeg
1 teaspoon ground cinnamon
1 teaspoon ground ginger
1 teaspoon salt
1 large egg
1 cup milk
¼ cup canola oil

1  Position the rack in the center of the oven and preheat to 425 degrees F. Lightly grease or line with paper baking cups twelve 2¾-inch muffin cups.

2  In a large bowl, blend together the flour, sugar, baking powder, nutmeg, cinnamon, ginger, and salt. In a medium bowl, beat the egg until foamy. Beat in the milk and oil. Combine the two mixtures, blending until the dry ingredients are just moistened.

3  Spoon the batter into the prepared muffin cups, filling each about three-quarters full. Bake for 15 to 20 minutes, or until a cake tester or wooden toothpick inserted into the center of a muffin comes out clean. Cool in the pan on a wire rack for 5 to 7 minutes. Serve warm, or invert onto the rack to cool completely.

# Spinach Muffins with Chick Peas

Makes: *11 to 12 muffins*

2 tablespoons butter or margarine
4 scallions (green onions),
    chopped fine
1 cup finely chopped fresh
    spinach leaves
1 tablespoon garlic powder
2 cups all-purpose flour
1 cup cornmeal
2 teaspoons baking powder
¼ teaspoon dried tarragon, crushed
One 15-ounce can chick peas,
    rinsed and drained
2 tablespoons grated Romano cheese
3 large eggs
1¼ cups milk
3 tablespoons butter or
    margarine, melted

1  Position the rack in the center
of the oven and preheat to 375
degrees F. Lightly grease or line
with paper baking cups twelve
2¾-inch muffin cups.

2  In a small skillet set over a
medium heat, melt the butter.
Add onion, spinach, and garlic
powder. Cook, stirring, until the
onion just starts to turn
translucent and the spinach is
wilted. Remove from the heat
and set aside.

3  In a large bowl, blend together
the flour, cornmeal, baking
powder, tarragon, chick peas,
and cheese. In a medium bowl,
beat the eggs until foamy. Beat
in the milk and butter. Stir in the
spinach mixture. Combine the
two mixtures, blending until the
dry ingredients are just
moistened.

4  Spoon the batter into the
prepared muffin cups, filling
each about three-quarters full.
Bake for 15 to 20 minutes, or
until a cake tester or wooden
toothpick inserted into the
center of a muffin comes out
clean. Cool in the pan on a wire
rack for 5 to 7 minutes. Serve
warm, or invert onto the rack to
cool completely.

# Strawberry Muffins

Makes: *12 to 14 muffins*

2¼ cups all-purpose flour
⅓ cup granulated sugar
1 tablespoon baking powder
½ teaspoon salt
2 large eggs
½ cup milk
1 teaspoon vanilla extract
1 cup sliced strawberries

**1** Position the rack in the center of the oven and preheat to 400 degrees F. Lightly grease or line with paper baking cups fourteen 2¼-inch muffin cups.

**2** In a large bowl, blend together the flour, sugar, baking powder, and salt. In a medium bowl, beat the eggs until thick and light-colored. Beat in the milk and vanilla extract. Stir in the strawberries. Combine the two mixtures, blending until the dry ingredients are just moistened.

**3** Spoon the batter into the prepared muffin cups, filling each about three-quarters full. Bake for about 15 to 20 minutes, or until a cake tester or wooden toothpick inserted into the center of a muffin comes out clean. Cool in the pan on a wire rack for 5 to 7 minutes. Serve warm, or invert onto the rack to cool completely.

# Sweet Potato-and-Marshmallow Surprise Muffins

Makes: *24 to 26 muffins*

3 cups all-purpose flour
2 teaspoons baking powder
1½ teaspoons baking soda
1 cup granulated sugar
2 teaspoons ground black pepper
½ teaspoon salt
3 large eggs
½ cup milk
1 cup plus 2 tablespoons canola oil
2 cups (about 2) sweet potatoes, mashed
78 miniature marshmallows

**1** Position the rack in the center of the oven and preheat to 375 degrees F. Lightly grease or line with paper baking cups twenty-six 2¼-inch muffin cups.

**2** In a large bowl, blend together the flour, baking powder, baking soda, sugar, pepper, and salt. In a medium bowl, beat the eggs until foamy. Beat in the milk, oil, and sweet potatoes. Combine the two mixtures, blending until the dry ingredients are just moistened.

**3** Drop 1 heaping tablespoon of the batter into each of the prepared muffin cups. Press two miniature marshmallows into the batter in each cup and top each with 1 heaping tablespoon of the remaining batter. (The muffin cups should be about two-thirds full). Press one or more miniature marshmallows onto the top of each muffin.

**4** Bake for 15 to 20 minutes, or until a cake tester or wooden toothpick inserted into the edge of a muffin (not into the marshmallows) comes out clean. Cool in the pan on a wire rack for 5 to 7 minutes. Serve warm, or invert onto the rack to cool completely.

# THE MUFFINS OF ST. PATRICK

MAKES: *5 to 6 muffins*

1½ cups all-purpose flour
¼ cup cornmeal
4 tablespoons powdered sugar
1½ teaspoons baking powder
1½ teaspoons baking soda
¼ teaspoon paprika
½ cup finely diced cooked ham
2 large eggs
3 tablespoons butter or margarine,
   melted
2 teaspoons prepared mustard
1 cup buttermilk or sour milk
Grated Swiss cheese for topping

**1** Position the rack in the center of oven and preheat to 400 degrees F. Lightly grease or line with paper baking cups six 3-inch muffin cups.

**2** In a large bowl, blend together the flour, cornmeal, sugar, baking powder, baking soda, paprika, and diced ham. In a medium bowl, beat the eggs until foamy. Beat in the butter, mustard, and buttermilk. Combine the two mixtures, blending until the dry ingredients are just moistened.

**3** Spoon the batter into the prepared muffin cups, filling each about three-quarters full. Bake for 20 to 25 minutes, or until a cake tester or wooden toothpick inserted into the center of a muffin comes out clean. Remove from the oven and sprinkle grated Swiss cheese on top of each muffin. Cool in the pan on a wire rack for 5 to 7 minutes. Serve warm, or invert onto the rack to cool completely.

# VARIETY COFFEE MUFFINS

MAKES: *11 to 12 muffins*

2 cups all-purpose flour
½ cup granulated sugar
1 tablespoon baking powder
¼ cup Dutch-processed cocoa powder
2 large eggs
6 tablespoons butter or margarine,
   melted
1 cup sour cream
1 cup evaporated milk
1 tablespoon instant coffee
freshly grated zest from two oranges

**1** Position the rack in the center of the oven and preheat to 400 degrees F. Lightly grease or line with paper baking cups twelve 2¾-inch muffin cups.

**2** In a large bowl, blend together the flour, sugar, baking powder, and cocoa powder. In a medium bowl, beat the eggs until thick and light-colored. Beat in the butter, sour cream, milk, coffee, and orange zest. Combine the two mixtures, blending until the dry ingredients are just moistened.

**3** Spoon the batter into the prepared muffin cups, filling each about three-quarters full. Press half an orange slice into each muffin. Bake for 15 to 20 minutes, or until a cake tester or wooden toothpick inserted into the center of a muffin comes out clean. Cool in the pan on a wire rack for 5 to 7 minutes. Serve warm, or invert onto the rack to cool completely.

# Veggie Muffins

Makes: *11 to 12 muffins*

2 cups all-purpose flour
2 tablespoons granulated sugar
1 tablespoon baking powder
½ cup finely chopped pitted olives
½ cup grated carrots
2 tablespoons fresh snipped chives
¼ teaspoon dried red pepper flakes
¼ teaspoon salt
1 large egg
¾ cup milk
¼ cup canola oil
1 small package (3 ounces)cream
    cheese, cut into 12 chunks

**1** Position the rack in the center of the oven and preheat to 400 degrees F. Lightly grease or line with paper baking cups twelve 2¾-inch muffin cups.

**2** In a large bowl, blend together the flour, sugar, baking powder, olives, carrots, chives, red pepper flakes, and salt. In a medium bowl, beat the egg, milk, and oil until smooth. Combine the two mixtures, blending until the dry ingredients are just moistened.

**3** Spoon the batter into the prepared muffin cups, filling each about three-quarters full. Press one chunk of cream cheese into the center of the batter in each muffin cup. Bake for 15 to 20 minutes, or until a cake tester or wooden toothpick inserted into the center of a muffin comes out clean. Cool in the pan on a wire rack for 5 to 7 minutes. Serve warm, or invert onto the rack to cool completely.

Serving suggestion: **Serve with a thick soup.**

# Yankee Maple Muffins

Makes: *12 to 14 muffins*

2 cups all-purpose flour
1 cup yellow cornmeal
1 tablespoon baking powder
2 large eggs
¼ cup packed light-brown sugar
1 cup milk
⅓ cup maple syrup
¼ cup butter or margarine, melted
½ cup crushed, canned pineapple,
    drained

**1** Position the rack in the center of the oven and preheat to 375 degrees F. Lightly grease or line with paper baking cups fourteen 2¾-inch muffin cups.

**2** In a large bowl, blend together the flour, cornmeal, and baking powder. In a medium bowl, beat the eggs until foamy. Beat in the sugar. Beat in the milk, syrup, butter, and pineapple. Combine the two mixtures, blending until the dry ingredients are just moistened.

**3** Spoon the batter into the prepared muffin cups, filling each about three-quarters full. Bake for 25 to 30 minutes, or until a cake tester or wooden toothpick inserted into the center of a muffin comes out clean. Remove from the oven and brush the top of each muffin with the melted butter. Cool in the pan on a wire rack for 5 to 7 minutes. Serve warm, or invert onto the rack to cool completely.

# Zucchini Muffins

Makes: *23 to 24 muffins*

2 cups all-purpose flour
1 cup granulated sugar
1 teaspoon baking soda
¼ teaspoon baking powder
1½ teaspoons ground cinnamon
1 cup golden raisins
½ cup chopped walnuts
½ teaspoon salt
2 large eggs
½ cup canola oil
1 tablespoon vanilla extract
2 cups shredded zucchini

**1** Position the rack in the center of the oven and preheat to 375 degrees F. Lightly grease or line with paper baking cups twenty-four 2¾-inch muffin cups.

**2** In a large bowl, blend together the flour, sugar, baking soda, baking powder, cinnamon, raisins, walnuts, and salt. In a medium bowl, beat the eggs until foamy. Beat in the oil and vanilla extract. Stir in zucchini. Combine the two mixtures, blending until the dry ingredients are just moistened.

**3** Spoon the batter into the prepared muffin cups, filling each about three-quarters full. Bake for 15 to 20 minutes, or until a cake tester or wooden toothpick inserted into the center of a muffin comes out clean. Cool in the pan on a wire rack for 5 to 7 minutes. Serve warm, or invert onto the rack to cool completely.

# APPLESAUCE BISCUITS

MAKES: *6 to 8 biscuits*

2 cups all-purpose flour
1 tablespoon baking powder
¼ teaspoon baking soda
1 teaspoon salt
3 tablespoons vegetable shortening, chilled
1 large egg
¼ cup sour cream
½ cup applesauce
½ cup grated cheese

**1** Position the rack in the center of the oven and preheat to 425 degrees F.

**2** In a large bowl, blend together the flour, baking powder, baking soda, and salt. Using a pastry blender or two knives scissor-fashion, cut in the shortening until the mixture resembles fine meal. In a small bowl, combine the egg, sour cream, and applesauce. (Do not beat.) Pour into the dry mixture all at one time and stir briefly until the dough holds together.

**3** Turn the dough out onto a lightly floured surface and knead 7 to 8 times. Using a rolling pin, roll the dough out to a thickness of ½ inch. Using a 2-inch round cutter, cut out as many biscuits as possible. Place the biscuits 1 inch apart on an ungreased baking sheet. Rework the scraps until all the biscuits are cut.

**4** Sprinkle the cheese over the top of the biscuits and bake for 10 to 12 minutes, or until the tops are golden brown. Serve warm.

# Bisquick® Cheese Biscuits

Makes: *4 to 6 biscuits.*

2¼ cups Bisquick® baking mix
⅔ cup white port wine
1½ cups shredded sharp Cheddar
  cheese

**1** Position the rack in the center of the oven and preheat to 425 degrees F.

**2** In a large bowl, combine the baking mix and wine and stir just until the dough holds together. (Do not overmix.) Stir in the cheese.

**3** Turn the dough out onto a lightly floured surface and knead 7 to 8 times. Using a rolling pin, roll the dough out to a thickness of ½ inch. Using a 2-inch round cutter, cut out as many biscuits as possible. Place the biscuits 1 inch apart on an ungreased baking sheet. Rework the scraps until all the dough is used and brush with the remaining butter. Bake for 10 to 12 minutes, or until the top of the biscuits are golden brown. Serve warm.

# Blackberry Biscuits

Makes: *6 to 8 biscuits*

1 cup all-purpose flour
¼ cup graham flour
1½ teaspoons baking powder
¼ cup granulated sugar
½ teaspoon salt
¼ cup heavy cream
½ cup berry-flavored yogurt
½ cup blackberries
  washed and dried

**1** Position the rack in the center of the oven and preheat to 425 degrees F.

**2** In a large bowl, blend together the two flours, baking powder, sugar, salt, cream, and yogurt, stirring just until the dough holds together. (Do not over-mix.) Stir in the blackberries.

**3** Turn the dough out onto a lightly floured surface and knead 7 to 8 times. Using a rolling pin, roll the dough out to a thickness of ½ inch. Using a 2-inch round cutter, cut out as many biscuits as possible. Place the biscuits 1 inch apart on an ungreased baking sheet. Rework the scraps until all the dough is used. Bake for 10 to 12 minutes, or until the top of the biscuits are golden brown. Serve warm.

# Buttermilk Biscuits

Makes: *10 to 12 biscuits*

## Camp Biscuits

Makes: *16 to 18 biscuits*

2 cups all-purpose flour
2½ teaspoons baking powder
¼ teaspoon baking soda
1 tablespoon granulated sugar
¼ teaspoon salt
6 tablespoons butter or margarine, chilled
¼ cup melted butter or margarine, melted (for brushing)
¾ cup buttermilk or sour milk

**1** Position the rack in the center of the oven and preheat to 425 degrees F.

**2** In a large bowl, blend together the flour, baking powder, baking soda, sugar, and salt. Using a pastry blender or two knives scissor-fashion, cut in the butter until the mixture resembles fine meal. Add the buttermilk all at one time and stir just until the dough holds together. (Do not overmix.)

**3** Turn the dough out onto a lightly floured surface and knead 7 to 8 times. Using a rolling pin, roll the dough out to a thickness of ½ inch. Using a 2-inch round cutter, cut out as many biscuits as possible. Place the biscuits 1 inch apart on an ungreased baking sheet. Rework the scraps until all the dough is used. Brush with the melted butter. Bake for 10 to 12 minutes, or until the top of the biscuits are golden brown. Serve warm.

2 cups all-purpose flour
3¾ teaspoons baking powder
1 teaspoon salt
6 tablespoons butter or margarine, at room temperature
¾ cup milk

**1** Lightly grease a skillet and preheat it over a low flame.

**2** In a large bowl, blend together the flour, baking powder, and salt. Using a pastry blender or two knives scissor-fashion, cut in the butter until the mixture resembles fine meal. Add the milk all at one time and stir just until the dough holds together. (Do not overmix.)

**3** Turn the dough out onto a lightly floured surface and knead 7 to 8 times. Using a rolling pin, roll the dough out to a thickness of ½ inch. Using a 2-inch round cutter or the top of a cup or glass, cut out as many biscuits as possible. Place the biscuits 1 inch apart on the prepared skillet (you may have to work in batches). Cook until the biscuits are light brown on the underside. Turn and brown on the other side. Serve at once.

# CHEDDAR CHEESE BISCUITS

MAKES: *6 to 8 biscuits*

2 cups all-purpose flour
4 teaspoons baking powder
2 teaspoons granulated sugar
½ teaspoon salt
2 tablespoons butter or margarine, at
  room temperature
1 large egg
¾ cup milk
½ cup grated Cheddar cheese

**1** Position the rack in the center of the oven and preheat to 425 degrees F.

**2** In a large bowl, blend together the flour, baking powder, sugar, and salt. In a medium bowl, beat the egg, butter, and milk together before stirring in the Cheddar cheese. Then combine the two mixes, blending just until the dough holds together. (Do not overmix.)

**3** Turn the dough out onto a lightly floured surface and knead 7 to 8 times. Using a rolling pin, roll the dough out to a thickness of ½ inch. Cut with a 1-inch round cutter. Place the biscuits 1 inch apart on an ungreased baking sheet. Rework the scraps until all the dough is used. Bake for 10 to 12 minutes, or until the top of the biscuits are golden brown. Serve warm.

# CHOPPED CHERRY BISCUITS

MAKES: *8 to 10 biscuits*

1½ cups all-purpose flour
1 tablespoon baking powder
1½ teaspoons granulated sugar
½ teaspoon cream of tartar
¼ cup finely chopped dried cherries
½ teaspoon salt
¼ cup vegetable shortening, chilled
½ cup milk
¾ cup butter or margarine, melted

**1** Position the rack in the center of the oven and preheat to 425 degrees F.

**2** In a large bowl, blend together the flour, baking powder, chopped dried cherries, sugar, salt, and cream of tartar. Using a pastry blender or two knives scissor-fashion, cut in the shortening until the mixture resembles fine meal. Pour the milk and ½ cup of the butter in all at one time and stir just until the dough holds together. (Do not overmix.)

**3** Turn the dough out onto a lightly floured surface and knead 7 to 8 times. Using a rolling pin, roll the dough out to a thickness of ½ inch. Using a 2-inch round cutter, cut out as many biscuits as possible. Place the biscuits 1 inch apart on an ungreased baking sheet. Rework the scraps until all the dough is used and brush with the remaining butter. Bake for 12 to 15 minutes, or until the top of the biscuits are golden brown. Serve warm.

# GRAHAM BISCUITS

MAKES: *8 to 10 biscuits*

2 cups graham flour
1 cup all-purpose flour
2 tablespoons baking powder
¾ teaspoon salt
½ cup vegetable shortening, chilled
1 cup milk

**1** Position the rack in the center of the oven and preheat to 425 degrees F.

**2** In a large bowl, blend together the two flours, baking powder, and salt. Using a pastry cutter or two knives scissor-fashion, cut in the shortening until the mixture resembles fine meal. Add the milk all at one time and stir just until the dough holds together. (Do not overmix.)

**3** Turn the dough out onto a lightly floured surface and knead 7 to 8 times. Using a rolling pin, roll the dough out to a thickness of ½ inch. Using a 2-inch round cutter, cut out as many biscuits as possible. Place the biscuits 1 inch apart on an ungreased baking sheet. Rework the scraps until all the dough is used. Bake for 10 to 12 minutes, or until the top of the biscuits are golden brown. Serve warm.

# GREEN TOMATO BISCUITS

MAKES: *14 to 16 biscuits*

1 cup all-purpose flour
1 cup whole-wheat flour
1 tablespoon baking powder
¼ cup grated Romano cheese
¾ teaspoon salt
2 large eggs
½ cup chopped green tomatoes
1 teaspoon wine vinegar
6 tablespoons butter or margarine, melted

**1** Position the rack in the center of the oven and preheat to 425 degrees F.

**2** In a large bowl, blend together the two flours, baking powder, cheese, and salt. In a medium bowl, blend together the egg, green tomatoes, vinegar, and butter. Then combine the two mixtures, blending until the dry ingredients are just moistened. (Do not overmix.)

**3** Turn the dough out onto a lightly floured surface and knead 7 to 8 times. Using a rolling pin, roll the dough out to a thickness of ½ inch. Using a 2-inch round cutter, cut out as many biscuits as possible. Place the biscuits 1 inch apart on an ungreased baking sheet. Rework the scraps until all the dough is used. Bake for 10 to 12 minutes, or until the top of the biscuits are golden brown. Serve warm.

# HEAVY CREAM BISCUITS

MAKES: *4 to 6 biscuits*

1¾ cups all-purpose flour
2½ teaspoons baking powder
1 cup heavy cream
½ teaspoon salt

**1** Position the rack in the center of the oven and preheat to 450 degrees F.

**2** In a large bowl, combine the flour, baking powder, cream, and salt and stir just until the dough holds together. (Do not overmix.)

**3** Turn the dough out onto a lightly floured surface and knead 7 or 8 times. Using a rolling pin, roll the dough out to a thickness of ½ inch. Using a 2-inch round cutter, cut out as many biscuits as possible. Place the biscuits 1-inch apart on an ungreased baking sheet. Rework the scraps until all the dough is used. Bake for 10 to 12 minutes, or until the top of the biscuits are golden brown. Serve warm.

# HONEY BISCUITS

MAKES: *10 to 12 biscuits*

**FILLING**
⅓ cup butter or margarine,
    at room temperature
¼ cup honey

**DOUGH**
2 cups all-purpose flour
4 teaspoons baking powder
½ tablespoon salt
¼ cup butter, or margarine
    at room temperature
⅔ cup milk
¼ cup sesame seeds

**1** Position the rack in the center of the oven and preheat to 325 degrees F.

**2** To make the filling, in a small bowl, beat together the butter and honey until smooth. Set aside.

**3** To make the dough, in a large bowl, blend together the flour, baking powder, and salt. Work in the butter until the mixture resembles fine meal. Add the milk all at one time and stir just until the dough holds together. (Do not overmix.)

**4** Turn the dough out onto a lightly floured surface and knead 7 to 8 times. Roll out to a rectangle ½ inch thick. Brush the rectangle with the honey butter. Roll the rectangle up jelly-roll fashion and cut into 1-inch slices. Place the slices on an ungreased baking sheet, and brush with any remaining honey butter. Sprinkle the tops of the biscuits with sesame seeds. Bake for 10 to 12 minutes, or until the top of the biscuits are golden brown. Serve warm.

# JALAPEÑO PEPPER–
# CHEESE BISCUITS

**MAKES:** *6 biscuits*

1 cup all-purpose flour
2 tablespoons cornmeal
1½ teaspoons baking powder
½ cup finely grated sharp
    Chedar cheese
2 tablespoons peeled and
    chopped tomato
1 teaspoon seeded, minced
    jalapeño pepper
½ teaspoon salt
½ cup milk

**1** Position the rack in the center of the oven and preheat to 425 degrees F.

**2** In a large bowl, blend together the flour, cornmeal, baking powder, cheese, tomatoes, peppers, and salt. Add the milk all at one time and stir just until the dough holds together. (Do not overmix.)

**3** Turn the dough out onto a lightly floured surface and knead 7 to 8 times. Divide the dough into 6 equal balls and place the balls on an ungreased baking sheet. Pat the balls into 3-inch rounds. Bake for 10 to 12 minutes, or until the top of the biscuits are golden brown. Serve warm.

# MASHED POTATO
# BISCUITS

**MAKES:** *10 to 12 biscuits*

1¼ cups all-purpose flour
1 teaspoon salt
½ cup chilled butter
4 large egg yolks
2 tablespoons sour cream
1 cup cold mashed potatoes

**1** Position the rack in the center of the oven and preheat to 425 degrees F.

**2** In a large bowl, blend together the flour and salt. Using a pastry blender or two knives scissor-fashion, cut in the butter until the mixture resembles fine meal. In a medium bowl, beat 3 of the egg yolks until foamy before beating in the sour cream and potatoes. Combine the two mixtures, blending until the dry ingredients are just moistened and the dough holds together. (Do not overmix.)

**3** Turn the dough out onto a lightly floured surface and knead 7 to 8 times. Using a rolling pin, roll the dough out to a thickness of ½ inch. Using a 2-inch round cutter, cut out as many biscuits as possible. Place the biscuits 1 inch apart on an ungreased baking sheet. Rework the scraps until all the dough is used. Brush the tops of the biscuits with the remaining egg yolk. Bake for 10 to 12 minutes, or until the top of the biscuits are golden brown. Serve warm.

# Patriotic Biscuits

**Makes:** *10 to 12 biscuits*

2 cups all-purpose flour
1 tablespoon baking powder
2 tablespoons granulated sugar
½ teaspoon salt
½ cup butter or margarine, at room
  temperature
¼ cup finely chopped cranberries
¼ cup finely chopped blueberries
1 large egg, lightly beaten
½ cup milk

**1**  Position the rack in the center of the oven and preheat to 425 degrees F.

**2**  In a large bowl, blend together the flour, baking powder, sugar, and salt. Work in the butter until the mixture resembles fine meal. Stir in the cranberries and blueberries. Add the egg and milk all at one time, and stir just until the dough holds together. (Do not overmix.)

**3**  Turn the dough out onto a lightly floured surface and knead 7 to 8 times. Using a rolling pin, roll the dough out to a thickness of ½ inch. Using a 2-inch round cutter, cut out as many biscuits as possible. Place the biscuits 1 inch apart on an ungreased baking sheet. Rework the scraps until all the dough is used. Bake for 10 to 12 minutes, or until the top of the biscuits are golden brown. Serve warm.

# Pepper Egg Biscuits

**Makes:** *10 to 12 biscuits*

3 cups all-purpose flour
4½ teaspoons baking powder
1 tablespoon granulated sugar
¾ teaspoon salt
½ cup chilled butter or margarine
1 large bell pepper, seeded and
  finely diced
1 large egg
¾ cup milk

**1**  Position the rack in the center of the oven and preheat to 425 degrees F.

**2**  In a large bowl, blend together the flour, baking powder, sugar, and salt. Using a pastry blender or two knives scissor-fashion, cut in the butter until the mixture resembles fine meal. Stir in the pepper. In a small bowl, whisk together the egg and milk. Combine the two mixtures, blending just until the dough holds together. (Do not overmix.)

**3**  Turn the dough out onto a lightly floured surface and knead 7 to 8 times. Using a rolling pin, roll the dough out to a thickness of ½ inch. Using a 2-inch round cutter, cut out as many biscuits as possible. Place the biscuits 1 inch apart on an ungreased baking sheet. Rework the scraps until all the dough is used. Bake for 10 to 12 minutes, or until the top of the biscuits are golden brown. Serve warm.

# Rum Biscuits

Makes: *10 to 12 biscuits*

# Sugarless Whole-Wheat Biscuits

Makes: *8 to 10 biscuits*

2 cups all-purpose flour
2 teaspoons baking powder
½ teaspoon salt
3 tablespoons butter or margarine, chilled
¾ cup milk
12 sugar cubes
¼ cup rum

**1** Position the rack in the center of the oven and preheat to 425 degrees F.

**2** In a large bowl, blend together the flour, baking powder, and salt. Using a pastry blender or two knives scissor-fashion, cut in the butter until the mixture resembles fine meal. Add the milk all at one time and stir just until the dough holds together. (Do not overmix.)

**3** Turn the dough out onto a lightly floured surface and knead 7 to 8 times. Using a rolling pin, roll the dough out to a thickness of ½ inch. Using a 2-inch round cutter, cut out as many biscuits as possible. Place the biscuits 1 inch apart on an ungreased baking sheet. Rework the scraps until all the dough is used. Push a sugar cube into the center of each biscuit. Spoon the rum evenly over the sugar cubes. Bake for 10 to 12 minutes, or until the top of the biscuits are golden brown. Serve warm.

1½ cups all-purpose flour
½ cup whole-wheat flour
1 tablespoon baking powder
½ teaspoon salt
⅓ cup vegetable shortening, chilled
¾ cup milk
Sesame seeds for sprinkling

**1** Position the rack in the center of the oven and preheat to 425 degrees F.

**2** In a large bowl, blend together the two flours, baking powder, and salt. Using a pastry blender or two knives scissor-fashion, cut in the shortening until the mixture resembles fine meal. Add the milk all at one time and stir just until the dough holds together. (Do not overmix.)

**3** Turn the dough out onto a lightly floured surface and knead 7 to 8 times. Using a rolling pin, roll the dough out to a thickness of ½ inch. Using a 2-inch round cutter, cut out as many biscuits as possible. Place the biscuits 1 inch apart on an ungreased baking sheet. Rework the scraps until all the dough is used. Sprinkle the tops of the biscuits with sesame seeds. Bake for 10 to 12 minutes, or until the top of the biscuits are golden brown. Serve warm.

## ALL-GRAIN SCONES

MAKES: *8 scones*

½ cup buttermilk
1 large egg
1 tablespoon honey
1 tablespoon molasses
¼ cup unprocessed bran
½ cup all-purpose flour
½ cup whole-wheat flour
¼ cup rye flour
⅓ cup rolled oats
¼ cup cornmeal
2 teaspoons baking powder
½ teaspoon baking soda
½ teaspoon salt
6 tablespoons chilled butter or
　margarine, diced

**1** Position the rack in the center of the oven and preheat to 400 degrees F. Lightly grease and flour a baking sheet.

**2** In a medium bowl, beat the buttermilk, egg, honey, and molasses until smooth. Stir in the bran. In a large bowl, blend together the three flours, rolled oats, cornmeal, baking powder, baking soda, and salt. Using a pastry blender or two knives scissor-fashion, cut the butter into the mixture until it resembles coarse meal. Gently stir in the wet ingredients until the dough just holds together.

**3** Transfer the dough to the prepared baking sheet and pat it into an 8-inch circle. Using a serrated knife, score into 8 wedges (do not cut all the way through the dough). Bake for 18 to 20 minutes, or until the top is golden. Remove from the oven and serve hot.

## APPLE–OATMEAL SCONES

MAKES: *8 scones*

1½ cups all-purpose flour
1 cup rolled oats
2½ teaspoons baking powder
⅓ cup packed brown sugar
½ teaspoon salt
½ cup chilled butter or margarine,
　diced
¾ cup chopped apples, unpeeled and
　cored
⅔ cup chopped pitted dates
1 large egg, beaten
¼ cup milk, plus more for brushing
　the scones
2 tablespoons molasses
1 teaspoon vanilla extract

**1** Position the rack in the center of the oven and preheat to 400 degrees F. Lightly grease and flour a baking sheet.

**2** In a large bowl, blend together the oats, baking powder, brown sugar, and salt. Using a pastry blender or two knives scissor-fashion, cut the butter into the mixture until it resembles coarse meal. Stir in the apples and dates. Add the egg, milk, molasses, and vanilla extract, stirring gently until the dough just holds together.

**3** Transfer the dough to the prepared baking sheet and pat it into an 8-inch circle. Using a serrated knife, score the dough into 8 wedges (do not cut all the way through the dough). Brush the top of the scone with milk and bake for 18 to 20 minutes, or until the top is golden brown. Remove from the oven and serve hot.

# Aunt Ethel's Aberdeen Scones

**Makes:** *4 large scones*

3 cups all-purpose flour
6 teaspoons baking powder
6 tablespoons granulated sugar
1 teaspoon salt
2 tablespoons chilled vegetable
   shortening
1 cup buttermilk
1 large egg, beaten

**1** In a large bowl, blend together the flour, baking powder, sugar, and salt. Using a pastry blender or two knives scissor-fashion, cut in the shortening until the mixture forms fine crumbs. Add the buttermilk and egg, stirring gently until the dough holds together.

**2** Turn the dough out onto a floured surface and pat it out to a thickness of ¾-inch. Cut the dough into four wedges.

**3** Preheat a large skillet over medium heat. Place the pieces, one at a time, in the heated skillet and fry until browned on both sides. Remove from the pan and serve hot.

# Blue Cheese-and-Golden Raisin Scones

**Makes:** *8 scones*

1 cup all-purpose flour
2 teaspoons baking powder
Dash of white pepper
¼ cup chilled butter or margarine
¼ cup crumbled blue cheese
¼ cup golden raisins
½ cup milk

**1** Position the rack in the center of the oven and preheat to 425 degrees F. Lightly grease and flour a baking sheet.

**2** In a large bowl, blend together the flour, baking powder, and pepper. Using a pastry blender or two knives scissor-fashion, cut in the butter until the mixture resembles coarse meal. Stir in the cheese and raisins. Add the milk, stirring gently until the dough holds together.

**3** Turn the dough out onto a lightly floured surface and knead a few times. Shape into a ball, place the ball on the prepared baking sheet, and pat into a ½-inch-thick circle. Using a serrated knife, score into 8 wedges (do not cut all the way through the dough). Bake for 10 to 15 minutes, or until golden brown. Remove from the oven and serve hot.

# Buckingham Palace Scones

**Makes:** *8 scones*

3½ cups all-purpose flour
1 tablespoon baking powder
½ cup granulated sugar, plus more
    for sprinkling over the scones
Pinch salt
¾ cup chilled butter or margarine
½ cup raisins
1 large egg, beaten
½ cup milk
1 large egg white, beaten

**1** Position the rack in the center of the oven and preheat to 350 degrees F. Lightly grease and flour a baking sheet.

**2** In a large bowl, blend together the flour, baking powder, ½ cup sugar, and salt. Using a pastry blender or two knives scissor-fashion, cut in the butter until the mixture resembles coarse meal. Stir in the raisins. Add the egg and milk, stirring gently until the dough holds together.

**3** Turn the dough out onto the prepared baking sheet, and pat it into a ½-inch-thick circle. Using a serrated knife, score into 8 wedges (do not cut all the way through the dough). Brush with the beaten egg white and sprinkle with granulated sugar. Bake for 10 to 12 minutes, or until the top is golden brown. Remove from the oven and serve hot.

# Cape Breton Scones

**Makes:** *16 scones*

2 cups all-purpose flour
1 tablespoon baking powder
¼ teaspoon baking soda
2 tablespoons granulated sugar, plus
    more for sprinkling over the
    scones
1 teaspoon salt
1 cup chopped raisins or currants
½ cup sour cream or yogurt
¼ cup canola oil
1 large egg, beaten
3 tablespoons milk, plus more for
    brushing the scones

**1** Position the rack in the center of the oven and preheat to 425 degrees F. Lightly grease and flour a baking sheet.

**2** In a large bowl, blend together the flour, baking powder, baking soda, the 2 tablespoons of sugar, salt, raisins, sour cream, oil, egg, and the 3 tablespoons of milk and stir gently until the dough holds together.

**3** Turn the dough out onto a lightly floured surface and knead gently until no longer sticky. Divide into two equal parts and form each into a ball. Place the balls on the prepared baking sheet and pat them into a 6-inch circles. Using a serrated knife, score each into 8 wedges (do not cut all the way through the dough). Brush the tops with milk and sprinkle with granulated sugar. Bake for 10 to 12 minutes, or until the tops are golden brown. Remove from the oven and serve hot.

# CHOCOLATE BROWNIE SCONES

**MAKES:** *8 scones*

3 ounces unsweetened chocolate, chopped
2 cups all-purpose flour
2¼ teaspoons baking powder
½ cup granulated sugar
¼ teaspoon salt
⅓ cup chilled butter or margarine, diced
½ cup chopped walnuts
⅓ cup milk
½ cup packed brown sugar
1 large egg
1½ teaspoons vanilla extract

**1** Position the rack in the center of the oven and preheat to 350 degrees F. Lightly grease and flour a baking sheet.

**2** In the top of a double boiler set over simmering water, melt the chocolate, stirring occasionally, until smooth. Set aside to cool slightly.

**3** In a large bowl, blend together the flour, baking powder, sugar, and salt. Using a pastry blender or two knives scissor-fashion, cut the butter into the mixture until it resembles coarse meal. Stir in the walnuts. In a small bowl, beat the milk, brown sugar, egg, and vanilla extract. Mix together until the sugar is dissolved. Stir in the melted chocolate. Combine the two mixtures, stirring gently until the dough holds together.

**4** Turn the dough out onto a lightly floured surface and pat it into a 7-inch circle. Place the circle on the prepared baking sheet and use a serrated knife to score the dough into 8 wedges (do not cut all the way through the dough). Bake for 18 to 20 minutes, or until the top is a darker brown. Remove from the oven and serve hot.

# CURRANT AND BRANDY SCONES

**MAKES:** *10 to 12 scones*

1 cup dried currants
3 tablespoons brandy
4 cups all-purpose flour
½ cup rice flour
2 teaspoons baking powder
½ teaspoon baking soda
¼ cup granulated sugar
1 cup chilled butter or margarine, diced
1 cup heavy cream

**1** In a cup, combine the currants and brandy and set aside to soak. In a large bowl, blend together the two flours, baking powder, baking soda, and sugar. Using a pastry blender or two knives scissor-fashion, cut the butter into the dry ingredients until the mixture resembles coarse meal. Add the currants and cream, stirring gently until the dough holds together.

**2** Gather the dough into a ball and wrap it in plastic wrap. Refrigerate until well chilled, about one hour.

**3** When ready to bake, position the rack in the center of the oven and preheat to 400 degrees F. Lightly grease and flour a baking sheet.

**4** Unwrap the dough and turn it out onto a floured surface. Roll the dough out to a thickness of ½-inch. Using a biscuit cutter, cut into 2-inch circles, reworking the scraps as you go. Place the circles 1 inch apart on the baking sheet. Bake for 13 to 15 minutes, or until golden brown. Remove from the oven and serve hot.

# ENGLISH CREAM SCONES

**MAKES:** *10 to 12 scones*

2 cups all-purpose flour
1 tablespoon baking powder
4 teaspoons granulated sugar, plus more for sprinkling over the scones
½ teaspoon salt
¼ cup chilled butter or margarine, diced
2 large eggs, beaten
½ cup sweet cream
1 beaten egg white

**1** Position the rack in the center of the oven and preheat to 375 degrees F. Lightly grease and flour a baking sheet.

**2** In a large bowl, blend together the flour, baking powder, the 4 teaspoons of sugar, and the salt. Using a pastry blender or two knives scissor-fashion, cut in the butter until the mixture resembles coarse meal. Add the egg and cream, stirring gently until the dough holds together.

**3** Turn the dough out onto a floured surface and knead several times before rolling out to a thickness of ½-inch. Using a biscuit cutter, cut the dough into 2-inch circles, reworking the scraps as you go. Place the circles 1 inch apart on the prepared baking sheet. Brush with the beaten egg white and sprinkle with sugar. Bake for 15 to 18 minutes, or until golden brown. Remove from the oven and serve hot.

# GINGER SCONES

MAKES: *12 scones*

# OLD-FASHIONED ORANGE SCONES

MAKES: *8 scones*

**DOUGH**
2¼ cups all-purpose flour
3½ teaspoons baking powder
½ cup granulated sugar
½ teaspoon salt
6 tablespoons minced crystallized ginger
1⅔ cups heavy cream

**TOPPING**
¼ teaspoon ground ginger for sprinkling
6 tablespoons granulated sugar for sprinkling

**1** Position the rack in the center of the oven and preheat to 425 degrees F. Lightly grease and flour a baking sheet.

**2** To make the dough, in a large bowl, blend together the flour, baking powder, sugar, salt, crystallized ginger, and cream and stir gently until the dough holds together.

**3** Turn the dough out onto a floured surface and knead several times before rolling out to a thickness of ½-inch. Using a biscuit cutter, cut the dough into 2-inch circles, reworking scraps as you go. Place the circles 1 inch apart on the prepared baking sheet.

**4** To make the topping, in a cup, combine the ground ginger and sugar. Sprinkle over the tops of the scones and bake for 10 to 15 minutes, or until golden brown. Remove from the oven and serve hot.

2 cups all-purpose flour
1 tablespoon baking powder
¼ cup powdered sugar
½ teaspoon salt
¼ cup chilled butter or margarine
1 teaspoon grated orange zest
¾ cup heavy cream
1 large egg, beaten
½ cup finely chopped golden raisins

**1** Position the rack in the center of the oven and preheat to 350 degrees F. Lightly grease and flour the bottom of a 6-inch round baking pan.

**2** In a large bowl, blend together the flour, baking powder, sugar, and salt. Using a pastry blender or two knives scissor-fashion, cut in the butter until the mixture resembles coarse meal. Add the orange zest, cream, egg, and raisins and stir gently until the dough holds together.

**3** Turn the dough out into the prepared baking pan and pat it down. Using a serrated knife, score the dough into 8 wedges (do not cut all the way through). Bake for 20 to 25 minutes, or until a golden brown. Remove from the oven and cool on a wire rack for about 5 to 7 minutes before serving warm.

# Parmesan and Cheddar Cheese Scones

MAKES: *8 scones*

2 cups all-purpose flour
2 teaspoons baking powder
Dash of ground cayenne
  pepper
¼ teaspoon salt
⅓ cup chilled butter or
  margarine, diced
3 tablespoons grated
  Parmesan cheese
1½ cups shredded Cheddar
  cheese
2 large eggs, beaten
⅓ cup milk

1 Position the rack in the center of the oven and preheat to 400 degrees F. Lightly grease and flour a baking sheet.

2 In a large bowl, blend together the flour, baking powder, cayenne, and salt. Using a pastry blender or two knives scissor-fashion, cut in the butter until the mixture resembles coarse meal. Stir in the Parmesan and Cheddar cheese. Add the eggs and milk, stirring gently until the dough holds together.

3 Turn the dough out onto the prepared baking sheet and pat it into an 8-inch circle. Using a serrated knife, score the dough into 8 wedges (do not cut all the way through the dough). Bake for 15 to 18 minutes, or until a golden brown. Remove from the oven and cool on a wire rack for 5 to 7 minutes before serving warm.

# RAISIN SCONES

**MAKES:** *16 to 18 scones*

3¼ cups all-purpose flour
1 tablespoon baking powder
5 tablespoons granulated sugar
1 teaspoon salt
6 tablespoons chilled butter or
    margarine, diced
1 cup golden raisins
1 cup milk

**1** Position the rack in the center of the oven and preheat to 425 degrees F. Lightly grease and flour a baking sheet.

**2** In a large bowl, blend together the flour, baking powder, sugar, and salt. Using a pastry blender or two knives scissor-fashion, cut in the butter until the mixture resembles coarse meal. Stir in the raisins. Add the milk and stir gently until the dough holds together.

**3** Turn the dough out onto a floured surface and knead several times before rolling it out to a thickness of ½-inch. Using a biscuit cutter, cut the dough into 2-inch circles, placing the circles 1½-inches apart on the prepared baking sheet. Bake for 8 to 10 minutes or until golden brown. Remove from the oven and serve hot.

# ROSEMARY SCONES

**MAKES:** *8 scones*

2¼ cups all-purpose flour
2 teaspoons baking powder
¼ teaspoon baking soda
1 teaspoon salt
½ cup cold butter or margarine, diced
1 teaspoon fresh minced rosemary
½ teaspoon grated lemon zest
⅓ cup buttermilk
1 large egg

**1** Position the rack in the center of the oven and preheat to 400 degrees F. Lightly grease and flour a baking sheet.

**2** In a large bowl, blend together the flour, baking powder, baking soda, and salt. Using a pastry blender or two knives scissor-fashion, cut in the butter until the mixture resembles coarse meal. Stir in the rosemary and lemon zest. In a small bowl, beat the buttermilk and egg until smooth. Combine the two mixtures, stirring gently until the dough holds together.

**3** Gather the dough into a ball and place it on the prepared baking sheet. Pat the dough into an 8-inch circle. Using a serrated knife, cut the circle into 8 wedges, cutting all the way through the dough. Separate the wedges slightly and bake for 13 to 15 minutes, or until the tops are lightly browned. Remove from the oven and serve hot.

# Scottish Oat Scones

MAKES: *8 scones*

1½ cups all-purpose flour
1¼ cups old-fashioned rolled oats
1 tablespoon baking powder
1 teaspoon cream of tartar
¼ cup granulated sugar
½ teaspoon ground nutmeg
½ teaspoon salt
1 large egg, beaten
⅓ cup milk
⅔ cup melted butter or margarine
½ cup golden raisins

**1** Position the rack in the center of the oven and preheat to 450 degrees F. Lightly grease and flour a baking sheet.

**2** In a large bowl, blend together the flour, oats, baking powder, cream of tartar, sugar, nutmeg, salt, egg, milk, butter, and raisins. Stir gently until the dough holds together.

**3** Gather the dough into a ball and transfer it to the prepared baking sheet. Pat the dough out into a ¾-inch-thick circle. Using a serrated knife, score into 8 wedges (do not cut all the way through) and bake for 10 to 12 minutes, or until golden brown. Remove from the oven and cool on a wire rack for 5 to 7 minutes before serving warm.

# Whole-Wheat Scones

MAKES: *4 scones*

1 cup whole-wheat flour
⅓ cup all-purpose flour
½ teaspoon baking powder
2 tablespoons wheat germ
2 tablespoons granulated sugar
¼ teaspoon salt
¼ cup chilled butter or margarine, diced
½ cup milk

**1** Position the rack in the center of the oven and preheat to 375 degrees F. Lightly grease and flour a baking sheet.

**2** In a large bowl, blend together the two flours, baking powder, wheat germ, sugar, and salt. Using a pastry blender or two knives scissor-fashion, cut in the butter until the mixture resembles coarse meal. Add the milk and stir gently until the dough holds together.

**3** Turn the dough out onto a floured surface and divide it into four equal pieces. Form each piece shape into a ball and place them on the prepared baking sheet. Pat each down into a 3-inch circle. Bake for 15 to 20 minutes, or until golden brown. Remove from the oven and cool on a wire rack for 5 to 7 minutes before serving warm or cooled.

# BASIC POPOVERS

MAKES: *10 to 12 popovers*

1 cup all-purpose flour
½ teaspoon salt
2 large eggs
1 cup milk
1 tablespoon butter or margarine,
  melted

**1** Position the rack in the center of the oven and preheat to 425 degrees F. Liberally grease a 12-cup muffin baking pan or 12 oven-proof custard cups. Place in the oven until needed.

**2** In a small bowl, blend together the flour and salt. In a medium bowl, beat the eggs until foamy. Beat in the milk and butter. Add the dry ingredients all at one time and beat until smooth.

**3** Spoon the batter into the hot cups, filling each about three-quarters full. Bake for 15 minutes (do not open the oven door). Reduce the heat to 375 degrees F and bake for an additional 20 to 25 minutes, or until the tops are firm to the touch and a deep golden brown.

**4** Turn off the oven, remove the popovers from the oven and prick the side of each popover with a fork. Return the popovers to the oven for an additional 5 minutes. Remove the popovers from the baking cups (run a knife around the edges of cups if necessary) and serve hot.

# CHEESY MORNING POPOVERS

MAKES: *6 to 8 popovers*

1⅓ cups all-purpose flour
½ cup shredded Swiss cheese
½ teaspoon salt
4 large eggs
⅔ cup milk
⅔ cup water

**1** Position the rack in the center of the oven and preheat to 425 degrees F. Liberally grease a 12-cup muffin baking pan or 12 oven-proof custard cups. Place in the oven until needed.

**2** In a small bowl, blend together the flour, cheese, and salt. In a medium bowl, beat the eggs until foamy. Beat in the milk and water. Add the dry ingredients all at one time and beat until smooth.

**3** Spoon the batter into the hot cups, filling each about three-quarters full. Bake for 15 minutes (do not open the oven door). Reduce the heat to 375 degrees F and bake for an additional 20 to 25 minutes, or until the tops are firm to the touch and a deep golden brown.

**4** Turn off the oven, remove the popovers from the oven and prick the side of each popover with a fork. Return the popovers to the oven for an additional 5 minutes. Remove the popovers from the baking cups (run a knife around the edges of cups if necessary) and serve hot.

# New England Family Popovers

Makes: *6 to 8 servings*

1 tablespoon butter or margarine
2 pounds tart apples, peeled, cored
    and diced
3 tablespoons granulated sugar
1 teaspoon vanilla extract
¼ teaspoon ground allspice
1 cup milk
2 large eggs, separated
1 cup all-purpose flour
¼ teaspoon salt

1 In a large oven-proof skillet set over medium heat, melt the butter. Add the apples and 2 tablespoons of the sugar. Cook, stirring frequently, for 15 to 20 minutes or until the apples are tender and most of the liquid has evaporated. Remove from the heat and stir in the vanilla extract and allspice. Set aside.

2 Position the rack in the center of the oven and preheat to 425 degrees F. In a medium bowl, beat the remaining tablespoon of sugar, the milk, egg yolks, flour, and salt until smooth. In a small bowl, beat the egg whites until stiff but not dry. Fold the egg whites into the yolk mixture.

3 Spoon the batter over the top of the apples in the pan. Bake for 20 minutes (do not open the oven door). Reduce the heat to 350 degrees F. and bake for an additional 10 to 15 minutes, or until the top of the popover is firm to the touch and golden brown. Remove the pan from the oven and cool it on a wire rack for 3 to 5 minutes before cutting into wedges and serving.

# Passover Popovers

Makes: *10 to 12 popovers*

4 large eggs
½ cup unsalted butter or margarine,
    melted
1 cup water
½ cup cake meal
½ cup matzo meal
¼ teaspoon salt

1 Position the rack in the center of the oven and preheat to 425 degrees F. Liberally grease a 12-cup muffin baking pan or 12 oven-proof custard cups. Place in the oven until needed.

2 In the container of a blender, combine the eggs, butter, water, cake meal, matzo meal, and salt and process on high for 3 to 4 seconds or until smooth.

3 Pour the batter into the hot cups, filling each about three-quarters full. Bake for 15 minutes (do not open the oven door). Reduce the heat to 375 degrees F and bake for an additional 20 to 25 minutes, or until the tops are firm to the touch and a deep golden brown.

4 Turn off the oven, remove the popovers from the oven and prick the side of each popover with a fork. Return the popovers to the oven for an additional 5 minutes. Remove the popovers from the baking cups (run a knife around the edges of cups if necessary) and serve hot.

# ALMOND BREAD

MAKES: *1 loaf*

# APPLE-AND-CHERRY BREAD

MAKES: *1 loaf*

1¼ cups sifted all-purpose flour
1½ teaspoons baking powder
¼ cup almond halves
⅛ teaspoon salt
⅓ cup granulated sugar
4 large eggs
2 tablespoons lemon juice
2 tablespoons melted butter or margarine

**1** Position the rack in the center of the oven and preheat to 375 degrees F. Lightly grease and flour an 8-inch square baking pan.

**2** In a large bowl, blend together the flour, baking powder, almonds, and salt. In a medium bowl, beat the sugar and eggs until smooth before beating in the lemon juice and butter. Combine the two mixtures, blending until the dry ingredients are moistened.

**3** Scrape the batter into the prepared baking pan and bake for 35 to 40 minutes, or until a cake tester or wooden toothpick inserted into the center of the bread comes out clean and the top is golden brown. Remove from the oven and cool in the pan on a wire rack for 5 to 10 minutes before cutting into squares and serving.

1½ cups whole-wheat flour
1 cup all-purpose flour
1 cup rolled oats
1 tablespoon baking powder
1½ teaspoons ground cinnamon
2 medium apples, peeled, cored, and finely chopped
1 cup candied cherry halves
½ cup golden raisins
1 teaspoon grated lemon or orange zest
4 large eggs
¾ cup milk
½ cup apple-flavored yogurt
¼ cup unsweetened frozen apple-juice concentrate, thawed

**1** Position the rack in the center of the oven and preheat to 350 degrees F. Lightly grease and flour a 9¼-by-5½-by-2¾-inch loaf pan.

**2** In a large bowl, blend together the two flours, oats, baking powder, cinnamon, apples, cherries, raisins, and lemon zest. In a medium bowl, beat the eggs until foamy before beating in the milk, yogurt, and apple juice. Combine the two mixtures, blending until the dry ingredients are thoroughly moistened.

**3** Scrape the batter into the prepared pan and bake for 55 to 60 minutes, or until a cake tester or wooden toothpick inserted into the center of the bread comes out clean and the top is golden brown. Remove the pan from the oven and cool on a wire rack for 5 to 10 minutes before removing the loaf from the pan.

# APRICOT–DATE BREAD

MAKES: *1 loaf*

1 cup all-purpose flour
½ cup whole-wheat flour
½ cup granulated sugar
2 teaspoons baking powder
¼ teaspoon baking soda
1 tablespoon grated orange zest
½ cup finely chopped dried apricots
½ cup finely chopped pitted dates
½ teaspoon salt
¾ cup milk or light cream, at room
     temperature
1 large egg
1 tablespoon melted butter or
     margarine

**1** Position the rack in the center of oven and preheat to 375 degrees F. Lightly grease and flour an 8½-by-4½-by-2½-inch loaf pan.

**2** In a large bowl, blend together the two flours, sugar, baking powder, baking soda, orange zest, apricots, dates, and salt. In a small bowl, beat the milk, egg, and butter until smooth. Combine the two mixtures, blending until the dry ingredients are just moistened.

**3** Scrape the batter into the prepared pan and bake for 40 to 45 minutes, or until a cake tester or wooden toothpick inserted into the center of the bread comes out clean and the top is golden brown. Remove from the oven and cool the pan on a wire rack for 5 to 10 minutes before removing the loaf from the pan.

# ASIAN RICE FLOUR BREAD

MAKES: *1 loaf*

1 cup millet flour
¾ cup rice flour
1 teaspoon baking soda
2 teaspoons cream of tartar
½ teaspoon salt
1 large egg
1 cup milk or goat's milk

**1** Position the rack in the center of the oven and preheat to 350 degrees F. Lightly grease and flour a 9-inch square baking pan.

**2** In a large bowl, blend together the 2 flours, baking soda, cream of tartar, and salt. In a medium bowl, beat the egg until foamy before beating in the milk. Combine the two mixtures, blending until the dry ingredients are moistened.

**3** Scrape the batter into the prepared pan and bake for 25 to 30 minutes, or until a cake tester or wooden toothpick inserted into the center of the bread comes out clean and the top is golden brown. Remove from the oven and cool the pan on a wire rack for 5 to 10 minutes before removing the loaf from the pan.

# AVOCADO BREAD

MAKES: *1 loaf*

2 cups all-purpose flour
1½ teaspoons baking powder
¼ cup granulated sugar
1 large egg
¼ cup melted butter or margarine
1 cup milk, at room temperature
1 medium avocado, pureed
1 cup toasted slivered almonds for
 topping

**1** Position the rack in the center of the oven and preheat to 350 degrees F. Lightly grease and flour an 8½-by-4½-by-2½-inch loaf pan.

**2** In a large bowl, blend together the flour, baking powder, and sugar. In a medium bowl, beat the egg until foamy before beating in the butter, milk, and avocado. Combine the two mixtures, blending until the dry ingredients are moistened.

**3** Scrape the batter into the prepared pan and bake for 45 to 50 minutes, or until a cake tester or wooden toothpick inserted into the center of the bread comes out clean and the top is golden brown. Remove from the oven and cool the pan on a wire rack for 5 to 10 minutes before removing the loaf from the pan. Sprinkle top with almonds.

# BACON–CORN BREAD

MAKES: *1 loaf*

8 ounces sliced bacon
2 cups all-purpose flour
1½ cups cornmeal
¼ cup granulated sugar
2 tablespoons baking powder
2 teaspoons salt
2 large eggs
1¼ cups milk
¼ cup vegetable oil

**1** In a large skillet, cook the bacon until crisp. Drain, reserving ½ cup of the drippings, and cool the bacon on paper towels. When cooled, crumble and set aside.

**2** Position the rack in the center of the oven and preheat to 400 degrees F. Lightly grease and flour a 9-inch square baking pan.

**3** In a large bowl, blend together the flour, cornmeal, sugar, baking powder, and salt. In a medium bowl, beat the eggs until foamy before beating in the milk, oil, and ½ cup reserved drippings. Combine the two mixtures, blending until the dry ingredients are just moistened.

**4** Scrape the batter into the prepared pan and sprinkle the crumbled bacon over the top. Bake for 20 to 25 minutes, or until a cake tester or wooden toothpick inserted into the center of the bread comes out clean and the top is golden brown. Remove from the oven and cool the pan on a wire rack for 5 to 10 minutes before cutting into squares and serving.

# Banana–Blueberry Bread

MAKES: *1 loaf*

1½ cups whole-wheat flour
½ cup all-purpose flour
½ cup rolled oats
2 teaspoons baking powder
½ teaspoon baking soda
½ cup fresh or frozen blueberries
2 large egg whites
¼ cup melted butter or margarine
1 cup mashed bananas
¾ cup frozen apple-juice concentrate, thawed

**1** Position the rack in the center of the oven and preheat to 325 degrees F. Lightly grease and flour an 8½-by-4½-by-2½-inch loaf pan.

**2** In a large bowl, blend together the two flours, oats, baking powder, and baking soda. Stir in the blueberries. In a medium bowl, beat the egg whites until stiff but not dry. Stir in the butter, bananas, and apple juice. Combine the two mixtures, blending until the dry ingredients are moistened.

**3** Scrape the batter into the prepared pan and bake for 50 to 55 minutes, or until a cake tester or wooden toothpick inserted into the center of the bread comes out clean and the top is golden brown. Remove from the oven and cool the pan on a wire rack for 5 to 10 minutes before removing the loaf from the pan.

# Banana Bread

MAKES: *1 loaf*

1½ cups all-purpose flour
1 cup oat flour
½ cup granulated sugar
1 teaspoon baking powder
1 teaspoon baking soda
1 teaspoon ground cinnamon
½ cup flaked coconut
½ teaspoon salt
2 large eggs
3 medium bananas, mashed
¼ cup canola oil
One 8-ounce can crushed pineapple (do not drain)
¼ cup shredded coconut for topping

**1** Position the rack in the center of the oven and preheat to 350 degrees F. Lightly grease and flour an 8½-by-4½-by-2½-inch loaf pan.

**2** In a large bowl, blend together the two flours, sugar, baking powder, baking soda, cinnamon, coconut, and salt. In a medium bowl, beat the eggs until foamy before beating in the bananas, oil, and pineapple with its juice. Combine the two mixtures, blending until the dry ingredients are moistened.

**3** Scrape the batter into the prepared pan and sprinkle the shredded coconut over the top. Bake for 45 to 50 minutes, or until a cake tester or wooden toothpick inserted into the center of the bread comes out clean and the top is golden brown. Remove from the oven and cool the pan on a wire rack for 5 to 10 minutes before removing the loaf from the pan.

# BIRDSEED BREAD

MAKES: *1 loaf*

# BOSTON BROWN BREAD

MAKES: *3 to 4 small loaves*

2 cups all-purpose flour
1 cup granulated sugar
2 teaspoons baking powder
¼ teaspoon ground cardamom
¼ cup poppy seeds
1 teaspoon grated lemon zest
2 large eggs
½ cup butter or margarine, melted
2 medium ripe bananas, mashed

1  Position the rack in the center of the oven and preheat to 350 degrees F. Lightly grease and flour an 8½-by-4½-by-2½-inch loaf pan.

2  In a large bowl, blend together the flour, sugar, baking powder, cardamom, poppy seeds, and lemon zest. In a medium bowl, beat the eggs until foamy before beating in the butter and bananas. Combine the two mixtures, blending until the dry ingredients are thoroughly moistened.

3  Scrape the batter into the prepared pan and bake for 45 to 50 minutes, or until a cake tester or wooden toothpick inserted into the center of the bread comes out clean and the top is golden brown. Remove from the oven and cool the pan on a wire rack for 5 to 10 minutes before removing the loaf from the pan.

1 cup all-purpose flour
1 cup graham flour
1 cup cornmeal
1½ teaspoons baking soda
1 teaspoon salt
¾ cup molasses
2 cups sour milk or buttermilk, warmed

1  Position the rack in the center of the oven and preheat to 350 degrees F. Lightly grease and flour four 5¼-by-3-by-2⅛-inch loaf pans.

2  In a large bowl, blend together the two flours, cornmeal, baking soda, and salt. In a medium bowl, blend the molasses and warmed sour milk until smooth. Combine the two mixtures, blending until the dry ingredients are just moistened.

3  Scrape the batter into the prepared baking pans and bake for 40 to 45 minutes, or until a cake tester or wooden toothpick inserted into the center of the bread comes out clean and the tops are golden brown. Remove from the oven and cool the pans on a wire rack for 5 to 10 minutes before removing the loaves from the pans.

# Brazil Nut–Apricot Bread

Makes: *1 loaf*

2 cups all-purpose flour
1 cup granulated sugar
1 tablespoon baking powder
¼ teaspoon baking soda
1 cup finely chopped Brazil nuts
½ cup chopped dried apricots
¾ teaspoon salt
1 large egg
2 tablespoons melted butter or
    margarine
¾ cup fresh-squeezed orange juice

**1** Position the rack in the center of the oven and preheat to 350 degrees F. Lightly grease and flour an 8¼-by-4½-by-2½-inch loaf pan.

**2** In a large bowl, blend together the flour, sugar, baking powder, baking soda, nuts, apricots, and salt. In a small bowl, beat the egg, butter, and orange juice until smooth. Combine the two mixtures, blending until the dry ingredients are just moistened.

**3** Scrape the batter into prepared pan and bake for 45 to 50 minutes, or until a cake tester or wooden toothpick inserted into the center of the bread comes out clean and the top is golden brown. Remove from the oven and cool the pan on a wire rack for 5 to 10 minutes before removing the loaf from the pan.

# Butterscotch–Hazelnut Bread

Makes: *1 loaf*

2 cups all-purpose flour
1 cup packed light-brown sugar
1 teaspoon baking powder
½ teaspoon baking soda
½ cup chopped hazelnuts
¼ teaspoon salt
1½ tablespoons melted butter or
    margarine
1 cup buttermilk or sour milk
1 large egg

**1** Position the rack in the center of the oven and preheat to 350 degrees F. Lightly grease and flour a 9¼-by-5¼-by-2¾-inch loaf pan.

**2** In a large bowl, blend together the flour, brown sugar, baking powder, baking soda, hazelnuts, and salt. In a medium bowl, beat the butter, buttermilk, and egg until smooth. Combine the two mixtures, blending until the dry ingredients are moistened.

**3** Scrape the batter into the prepared pan and bake for 55 to 60 minutes, or until a cake tester or wooden toothpick inserted into the center of the bread comes out clean and the top is golden brown. Remove from the oven and cool the pan on a wire rack for 5 to 10 minutes before removing the loaf from the pan.

# CARAWAY–BEER BREAD

MAKES: *1 loaf*

2 cups whole-wheat flour
1 cup all-purpose flour
1 cup granulated sugar
4 teaspoons baking powder
1 teaspoon baking soda
3 tablespoons caraway seeds
1 teaspoon salt
2 large eggs
½ cup packed light-brown sugar
1¼ cups beer, at room temperature
½ cup maple syrup, slightly warmed

**1** Position the rack in the center of the oven and preheat to 350 degrees F. Lightly grease and flour a 9¼-by-5¼-by-2¾-inch loaf pan.

**2** In a large bowl, blend together the two flours, granulated sugar, baking powder, baking soda, seeds, and salt. In a small bowl, beat the eggs, brown sugar, beer, and maple syrup until smooth. Combine the two mixtures, blending until the dry ingredients are moistened.

**3** Scrape the batter into the prepared pan and bake for 55 to 60 minutes, or until a cake tester or wooden toothpick inserted into the center of the bread comes out clean and the top is golden brown. Remove from the oven and cool the pan on a wire rack for 5 to 10 minutes before removing the loaf from the pan.

SERVING SUGGESTION: Serve with a cold beer and thinly sliced cheese of choice.

# CARDAMOM–HONEY BREAD

MAKES: *1 loaf*

1 cup all-purpose flour
1 cup whole-wheat flour
2½ cups oat or wheat bran
2 teaspoons baking powder
1 teaspoon baking soda
1 teaspoon ground cardamom
¼ teaspoon salt
4 large eggs
½ cup warmed honey
½ cup canola oil
¼ teaspoon vanilla extract
2 cups unsweetened applesauce

**1** Position the rack in the center of the oven and preheat to 350 degrees F. Lightly grease and flour a 9¼-by-5¼-by-2¾-inch loaf pan.

**2** In a large bowl, blend together the two flours, bran, baking powder, baking soda, salt, and cardamom. In a medium bowl, beat the eggs until foamy before beating in the honey, oil, and vanilla extract. Stir in the applesauce. Combine the two mixtures, blending until the dry ingredients are moistened.

**3** Scrape the batter into the prepared pan and bake for 55 to 60 minutes, or until a cake tester or wooden toothpick inserted into the center of the bread comes out clean and the top is golden brown. Remove the pan from the oven and cool on a wire rack for 5 to 10 minutes before removing the loaf from the pan.

# Cheddar Spoon Bread

**Makes:** *1 loaf*

4 large eggs, separated
2 cups milk
1 cup cornmeal
2 cups (8 ounces) Kraft® sharp
   Cheddar cheese, grated
½ cup margarine
1 teaspoon salt
Pinch ground cayenne

**1** Position the rack in the center of the oven and preheat to 375 degrees F. Lightly grease and flour a 2-quart casserole dish.

**2** In a medium bowl, beat the egg whites until stiff but not dry. Set aside. In a medium saucepan set over medium heat, heat the milk until bubbles start to form around the edges. Add the cornmeal and cook, stirring constantly, until the mixture is very thick and smooth. Remove from the heat and quickly stir in the cheese, margarine, salt, and cayenne, stirring until smooth. Stir in egg yolks. Fold in the egg whites.

**3** Pour the mixture into the prepared baking dish and bake for 35 to 40 minutes, or until the top is golden brown. Remove the casserole from the oven and serve immediately.

# Chocolate Banana Bread

**Makes:** *1 loaf*

½ cup all-purpose flour
¾ cup whole-wheat flour
½ cup rolled oats, processed to a
   powder in a food processor
1¼ teaspoons baking powder
½ teaspoon baking soda
½ cup Dutch-processed cocoa powder
½ teaspoon salt
⅔ cup granulated sugar
⅓ cup butter or margarine, at room
   temperature
2 large eggs
2 tablespoons heavy cream or milk
1 teaspoon chocolate or vanilla extract
1 cup mashed ripe bananas

**1** Position the rack in the center of the oven and preheat to 350 degrees F. Lightly grease and flour an 8½-by-4½-by-2½-inch loaf pan.

**2** In a large bowl, blend the two flours, oats, baking powder, baking soda, cocoa powder, and salt. In a medium bowl, beat the sugar and butter together until light and fluffy. Beat in the eggs, one at a time, beating vigorously after each addition. Beat in the cream, chocolate extract, and bananas. Combine the two mixtures, blending until the dry ingredients are moistened.

**3** Scrape the batter into the prepared pan and bake for 40 to 45 minutes, or until a cake tester or wooden toothpick inserted into the center of the bread comes out clean and the top is golden brown. Remove from the oven and cool the pan on a wire rack for 5 to 10 minutes before removing the loaf from the pan.

# CHOCOLATE TEA BREAD

**MAKES:** *6 to 8 servings*

2 cups all-purpose flour
2 teaspoons baking powder
¼ teaspoon baking soda
¼ teaspoon salt
2 teaspoons ground cinnamon
1 teaspoon ground ginger
1½ ounces unsweetened chocolate, grated
⅓ cup vegetable shortening
2 large eggs
¼ cup granulated sugar
¼ cup packed light-brown sugar
¼ cup dark molasses
½ cup milk

**1** Position the rack in the center of the oven and preheat to 350 degrees F. Lightly grease a 13-by-9-inch baking pan.

**2** In a large bowl, blend together the flour, baking powder, baking soda, salt, and spices. In the top of a double boiler set over simmering water, melt the chocolate and shortening, stirring until smooth. Remove from the heat and beat in the eggs, one at a time, beating vigorously after each addition. Beat in the sugars, molasses, and milk. Combine the two mixtures, blending until the dry ingredients are moistened.

**3** Spoon the batter into the prepared baking pan. Bake for 20 to 25 minutes, or until a cake tester or wooden toothpick inserted into the cake comes out clean and the top is dark brown. Remove the pan from the oven and cool on a wire rack for 5 to 7 minutes before removing loaf from the pan. Sprinkle with powdered sugar and serve warm or cooled.

# CHRISTMAS FRUIT BREAD

**MAKES:** *1 loaf*

2½ cups sifted all-purpose flour
4 teaspoons baking powder
1½ cups mixed candied fruit
¼ cup chopped seedless raisins
¾ cup chopped walnuts
¼ teaspoon salt
½ cup butter-flavored vegetable shortening
¾ cup granulated sugar
3 large eggs
3 medium bananas, mashed
½ cup orange juice

**1** Position the rack in the center of the oven and preheat to 350 degrees F. Lightly grease an 8½-by-4½-by-2½-inch loaf pan.

**2** In a large bowl, blend together the flour, baking powder, fruit, raisins, walnuts, and salt. In a medium bowl, beat the shortening and sugar together until light and fluffy before beating in the eggs, one at a time, beating vigorously after each addition. Beat in the bananas and orange juice. Combine the two mixtures, blending until the dry ingredients are well moistened.

**3** Scrape the batter into the prepared pan and bake for 45 to 50 minutes, or until a cake tester or wooden toothpick inserted into the center of the bread comes out clean and the top is golden brown. Remove from the oven and cool the pan on a wire rack for 5 to 10 minutes before removing the loaf from the pan.

# CREAM CHEESE BREAD

MAKES: *2 loaves*

2 cups all-purpose flour
1¼ teaspoons baking powder
1 teaspoon salt
One 8-ounce package cream cheese,
  at room temperature
1 cup butter or margarine, at room
  temperature
1 cup granulated sugar
3 large eggs

**1** Position the rack in the center of the oven and preheat to 350 degrees F. Lightly grease and flour two 8½-by-4½-by-2½-inch loaf pans.

**2** In a large bowl, blend together the flour, baking powder, and salt. In a medium bowl, beat the cheese, butter, and sugar together until smooth. Beat in the eggs, one at a time, beating vigorously after each addition. Combine the two mixtures, blending until the dry ingredients are well moistened.

**3** Scrape the batter into the prepared pans and bake for 45 to 50 minutes, or until a cake tester or wooden toothpick inserted into the center of the bread comes out clean and the tops are golden brown. Remove from the oven and cool the pans on a wire rack for 5 to 10 minutes before removing the loaves from the pans.

# ENRICHED PRUNE BREAD

MAKES: *1 loaf*

1 package (12 ounces) pitted prunes,
  coarsely chopped
1 cup freshly squeezed orange juice
⅔ cup granulated sugar
¼ cup butter or margarine, at room
  temperature
⅓ cup Triple Sec liqueur
1 teaspoon lemon or orange extract
1½ cups all-purpose flour
½ cup whole-wheat flour
1 teaspoon baking powder
1 teaspoon baking soda
¾ teaspoon ground cinnamon
¼ teaspoon ground cloves
Coarsely grated orange zest for
  topping

**1** Position the rack in the center of the oven and preheat to 350 degrees F. Lightly grease and flour an 8½-by-4½-by-2½-inch loaf pan.

**2** In a medium saucepan, combine the prunes, orange juice, sugar, and butter and set over medium heat. Cook until bubbles form around the edges of the pan. Remove from the heat and stir in the Triple Sec and lemon extract. Set aside to cool.

**3** In a large bowl, blend together the two flours, baking powder, baking soda, cinnamon, and cloves. Combine the dry ingredients with the prune mixture, blending until the dry ingredients are moistened.

**4** Scrape the batter into the prepared pan and sprinkle the orange zest over the top. Bake for 45 to 50 minutes, or until a cake tester or wooden toothpick inserted into the center of the bread comes out clean and the top is golden brown. Remove from the oven and cool the pan on a wire rack for 5 to 10 minutes before removing the loaf from the pan.

# Grape Nut–Apricot Bread

MAKES: *1 loaf*

2 cups hot scalded milk
1 cup Grape Nuts
1 cup finely chopped dried apricots
3 cups all-purpose flour
½ cup granulated sugar
4 teaspoons baking powder
1½ teaspoons salt
1 large egg
3 tablespoons melted butter or
    margarine

**1** Position the rack in the center of the oven and preheat to 350 degrees F. Lightly grease and flour a 9¼-by-5¼-by-2¾-inch loaf pan.

**2** In a small bowl, combine the milk, grape nuts, and apricots. Set aside to cool.

**3** In a large bowl, blend together the flour, sugar, baking powder, and salt. In a medium bowl, beat the egg until foamy before beating in the butter. Stir in the cooled grape nut mixture. Combine the wet and dry mixtures, blending until the dry ingredients are thoroughly moistened.

**4** Scrape the batter into the prepared pan and bake for 55 to 60 minutes, or until a cake tester or wooden toothpick inserted into the center of the bread comes out clean and the top is golden brown. Remove from the oven and cool the pan on a wire rack for 5 to 10 minutes before removing the loaf from the pan.

# Herbed Tomato Bread

MAKES: *1 loaf*

3 cups all-purpose flour
2½ teaspoons baking powder
½ teaspoon baking soda
2 tablespoons snipped fresh tarragon
1 tablespoon snipped fresh parsley
1 tablespoon granulated sugar
1 cup finely grated Cheddar cheese
½ teaspoon salt
2 large eggs
1 cup milk
¼ cup canola oil
2 tablespoons tomato paste
1 small yellow onion, finely chopped
1 teaspoon ketchup
½ cup grated Provolone cheese for
    topping

**1** Position the rack in the center of the oven and preheat to 350 degrees F. Lightly grease and flour a 9¼-by-5¼-by-2¾-inch loaf pan.

**2** In a large bowl, blend together the flour, baking powder, baking soda, tarragon, parsley, sugar, cheese, and salt. In a medium bowl, beat the eggs until foamy before beating in the milk, oil, tomato paste, onion, and ketchup. Combine the two mixtures, blending until the dry ingredients are moistened.

**3** Scrape the batter into the prepared pan and sprinkle the Provolone over the top. Bake for 55 to 60 minutes, or until a cake tester or wooden toothpick inserted into the center of the bread comes out clean and the top is golden brown. Remove from the oven and cool the pan on a wire rack for 5 to 10 minutes before removing the loaf from the pan.

# Hominy Bread

MAKES: *1 loaf*

# Italian-Style Prosciutto Bread

MAKES: *1 loaf*

2 cups cold cooked hominy
1½ tablespoons melted vegetable
   shortening
¼ teaspoon salt
2 large eggs, separated
1½ cups milk

**1** Position the rack in the center of the oven and preheat to 400 degrees F. Lightly grease and flour an 8-inch square baking pan.

**2** In a large bowl, combine the hominy, shortening, and salt. In a medium bowl, beat the egg yolks and milk until smooth before stirring in the hominy mixture. In a small bowl, beat the egg whites until stiff but not dry and fold into the hominy mixture.

**3** Scrape the batter into the prepared pan and bake for 55 to 60 minutes, or until a cake tester or wooden toothpick inserted into the center of the bread comes out clean and the top is golden brown. Remove from the oven and cool the pan on a wire rack for 5 to 10 minutes before cutting the bread into squares.

2½ cups all-purpose flour
1¼ teaspoons baking powder
½ teaspoon baking soda
5 slices Parma ham (Prosciutto),
   chopped
⅓ cup chopped sun-dried tomatoes
2 tablespoons snipped fresh basil
1½ teaspoons garlic powder
1 large egg
½ cup light olive oil
1¼ cups buttermilk or sour milk
Freshly ground black pepper to taste
Shredded Provolone cheese for
   topping

**1** Position the rack in the center of the oven and preheat to 350 degrees F. Lightly grease and flour a 9-inch square baking pan.

**2** In a large bowl, blend together the flour, baking powder, baking soda, ham, tomatoes, basil, and garlic powder. In a medium bowl, beat the egg, oil, and buttermilk until smooth. Combine the two mixtures, blending until the dry ingredients are moistened.

**3** Scrape the batter into the prepared pan and sprinkle with Provolone cheese. Bake for 40 to 45 minutes, or until a cake tester or wooden toothpick inserted into the center of the bread comes out clean and the top is golden brown. Remove from the oven and cool in the pan on a wire rack for 5 to 10 minutes before removing the loaf from the pan.

# MARBLEIZED CHOCOLATE LOAF

*MAKES: 1 loaf*

1¼ cups all-purpose flour
¾ teaspoon baking powder
¾ teaspoon baking soda
1 tablespoon grated orange zest
1 cup butter-flavored vegetable shortening
1 cup granulated sugar
3 large eggs
1 cup chocolate-flavored yogurt or plain sour cream
2 teaspoons chocolate or orange extract
2 ounces (2 squares) unsweetened chocolate, melted
⅓ cup crème de cacao

**1** Position the rack in the center of the oven and preheat to 350 degrees F. Lightly grease and flour an 8½-by-4½-by-2½-inch loaf pan.

**2** In a large bowl, blend together the flour, baking powder, baking soda, and orange zest. In a medium bowl, beat the shortening and sugar until light and fluffy. Beat in the eggs, one at a time, beating vigorously after each addition. Beat in ¾ cup of the yogurt and the chocolate extract. Scrape the batter into the prepared pan.

**3** In a small bowl, combine the remaining ¼ cup of yogurt, the melted chocolate, and crème de cacao and beat until smooth. Spoon over the top of the mixture in the pan, and using a knife or spatula, swirl it back and forth several times to make swirls throughout the batter.

**4** Bake for 45 to 50 minutes, or until a cake tester or wooden toothpick inserted into the center of the bread comes out clean and the top is dark brown. Remove from the oven and cool the pan on a wire rack for 10 minutes before removing the loaf from the pan. Transfer the loaf to the rack to cool completely.

# Natural Spelt Bread

Makes: *1 loaf*

3½ cups spelt flour
2 tablespoons baking soda
½ teaspoon vitamin C crystals
½ cup natural unsweetened
    applesauce
1¼ cups water

**1** Position the rack in the center of the oven and preheat to 350 degrees F. Lightly grease and flour a 9¼-by-5¼-by-2¾-inch loaf pan.

**2** In a large bowl, blend together the flour, baking soda, vitamin C, applesauce, and water, blending until the dry ingredients are moistened.

**3** Scrape the batter into the prepared pan and bake for 35 to 40 minutes, or until a cake tester or wooden toothpick inserted into the center of the bread comes out clean and the top is golden brown. Remove from the oven and cool in the pan on a wire rack before removing the loaf from the pan and transferring it to the rack to cool completely. Refrigerate until slicing and serving.

# Orange Marmalade Nut Bread

Makes: *1 loaf*

2 cups all-purpose flour
¾ cup graham flour
2 teaspoons baking powder
½ teaspoon baking soda
½ cup chopped walnuts
½ teaspoon salt
½ cup butter or margarine, at room
    temperature
½ cup packed light-brown sugar
2 large eggs
One 10-ounce jar orange marmalade
½ cup freshly squeezed orange juice

**1** Position the rack in the center of the oven and preheat to 350 degrees F. Lightly grease and flour an 8½-by-4½-by-2½-inch loaf pan.

**2** In a large bowl, blend together the two flours, baking powder, baking soda, walnuts, and salt. In a medium bowl, beat the butter and brown sugar until smooth before beating in the eggs, one at a time, beating vigorously after each addition. Beat in the marmalade and juice. Combine the two mixtures, blending until the dry ingredients are moistened.

**3** Scrape the batter into the prepared pan and bake for 55 to 60 minutes, or until a cake tester or wooden toothpick inserted into the center of the bread comes out clean and the top is golden brown. Remove from the oven and cool the pan on a wire rack for 5 to 10 minutes before removing the loaf from the pan.

# Peanut Butter–Bacon Bread

**Makes:** *1 loaf*

2 cups all-purpose flour
1 cup granulated sugar
1 tablespoon baking powder
1 cup crumbled
    crisply cooked bacon, plus more
    for topping the bread
1 cup coarsely chopped unsalted
    peanuts
½ teaspoon salt
1 large egg
1 tablespoon melted butter or
    margarine
1 cup milk
1 cup peanut butter
Honey for brushing

**1** Position the rack in the center of the oven and preheat to 350 degrees F. Lightly grease and flour an 8½-by-4½-by-2½-inch loaf pan.

**2** In a large bowl, blend together the flour, sugar, baking powder, one cup crumbled bacon, peanuts, and salt. In a medium bowl, beat the egg until foamy before beating in the butter, milk, and peanut butter. Combine the two mixtures, blending until the dry ingredients are moistened.

**3** Scrape the batter into the prepared pan and bake for 45 to 50 minutes, or until a cake tester or wooden toothpick inserted into the center of the bread comes out clean and the top is golden brown. Remove from the oven and cool the pan on a wire rack for 5 to 10 minutes before removing the loaf from the pan. Brush the loaf with honey and sprinkle with additional crumbled bacon.

# Pineapple–Nut Bread

**Makes:** *1 loaf*

2 cups all-purpose flour
2 teaspoons baking powder
¼ teaspoon baking soda
2 tablespoons granulated sugar
½ teaspoon ground cardamom
¾ cup chopped chestnuts or black
    walnuts
½ cup finely chopped seedless
    raisins
2 large eggs
¾ cup packed dark-brown sugar
3 tablespoons melted butter or
    margarine
One 8-ounce can crushed pineapple,
    undrained

**1** Position the rack in the center of the oven and preheat to 350 degrees F. Lightly grease and flour an 8½-by-4½-by-2½-inch loaf pan.

**2** In a large bowl, blend together the flour, baking powder, baking soda, granulated sugar, cardamom, chestnuts, and raisins. In a medium bowl, beat the eggs until foamy before beating in the brown sugar and butter. Stir in the pineapple. Combine the two mixtures, blending until the dry ingredients are thoroughly moistened.

**3** Scrape the batter into the prepared pan and bake for 55 to 60 minutes, or until a cake tester or wooden toothpick inserted into the center of the bread comes out clean and the top is golden brown. Remove from the oven and cool the pan on a wire rack for 5 to 10 minutes before removing the loaf from the pan.

# PLANTATION HERB BREAD

MAKES: *1 loaf*

2 cups all-purpose flour
1 tablespoon baking powder
1 cup cooked brown or wild rice
¼ teaspoon dried crushed thyme
½ teaspoon dried crushed basil
¼ teaspoon dried crushed parsley
¼ cup grated Parmesan or Romano
  cheese
2 large eggs
1 cup milk
3 tablespoons melted butter or
  margarine

**1** Position the rack in the center of the oven and preheat to 350 degrees F. Lightly grease and flour a 9¼-by-5¼-by-2¾-inch loaf pan.

**2** In a large bowl, blend together the flour, baking powder, rice, herbs, and cheese. In a medium bowl, beat the eggs until foamy before beating in the milk and butter. Combine the two mixtures, blending until the dry ingredients are well moistened.

**3** Scrape the batter into the prepared pan and bake for 55 to 60 minutes, or until a cake tester or wooden toothpick inserted into the center of the bread comes out clean and the top is golden brown. Remove from the oven and cool the pan on a wire rack for 5 to 10 minutes before removing the loaf from the pan.

# QUICK FRUIT BREAD

MAKES: *1 loaf*

1 cup all-purpose flour
1 cup whole-wheat flour
½ cup soy flour
½ cup oat bran
1 teaspoon baking soda
1 cup chopped nuts (optional)
½ teaspoon salt
¼ cup butter or margarine, at room
  temperature
½ cup granulated sugar
1 large egg
¼ cup fresh juice or berry-flavored
  liqueur
1 cup fruit pulp
1 cup sour milk or buttermilk

**1** Position the rack in the center of the oven and preheat to 350 degrees F. Lightly grease and flour a 9¼-by-5¼-by-2¾-inch loaf pan.

**2** In a large bowl, blend together the three flours, oat bran, baking soda, nuts, and salt. In a medium bowl, beat the butter and sugar until light and fluffy. Beat in the egg, juice, pulp, and sour milk. Combine the two mixtures, blending until the dry ingredients are well moistened.

**3** Scrape the batter into the prepared pan and bake for 55 to 60 minutes, or until a cake tester or wooden toothpick inserted into the center of the bread comes out clean and the top is golden brown. Remove from the oven and cool the pan on a wire rack for 5 to 10 minutes before removing the loaf from the pan.

# Rhubarb Bread

Makes: *1 loaf*

# Tangerine Tea Bread

Makes: *1 loaf*

2½ cups all-purpose flour
1 teaspoon baking soda
1½ cups diced fresh rhubarb
1½ cups chopped walnuts or pecans
1 teaspoon salt
1 large egg
1½ cups packed brown sugar
⅔ cup canola oil
1 cup buttermilk or sour milk
1 teaspoon vanilla extract

**1** Position the rack in the center of the oven and preheat to 350 degrees F. Lightly grease and flour an 8½-by-4½-by-2½-inch loaf pan.

**2** In a large bowl, blend together the flour, baking soda, rhubarb, walnuts, and salt. In a medium bowl, beat the egg and brown sugar until smooth before beating in the oil, sour milk, and vanilla extract. Combine the two mixtures, blending until the dry ingredients are thoroughly moistened.

**3** Scrape the batter into the prepared pan and bake for 45 to 50 minutes, or until a cake tester or wooden toothpick inserted into the center of the bread comes out clean and the top is golden brown. Remove from the oven and cool the pan on a wire rack for 5 to 10 minutes before removing the loaf from the pan.

1½ cups all-purpose flour
½ cup graham flour
2½ teaspoons baking powder
¼ teaspoon baking soda
3 tablespoons finely minced tangerine peel
½ cup chopped pecans or macadamia nuts
1 teaspoon salt
1 large egg
½ cup freshly squeezed tangerine juice
½ cup milk or light cream
¼ cup melted butter or margarine

**1** Position the rack in the center of the oven and preheat to 350 degrees F. Lightly grease and flour an 8½-by-4½-by-2½-inch loaf pan.

**2** In a large bowl, blend together the two flours, baking powder, baking soda, peel, pecans, and salt. In a small bowl, beat the egg until foamy before beating in the juice, milk, and butter. Combine the two mixtures, blending until the dry ingredients are moistened.

**3** Scrape the batter into the prepared pan and bake for 55 to 60 minutes, or until a cake tester or wooden toothpick inserted into the center of the bread comes out clean and the top is golden brown. Remove from the oven and cool the pan on a wire rack for 5 to 10 minutes before removing the loaf from the pan.

# Three-Grain Bread

MAKES: *1 loaf*

1 cup graham flour
1 cup rye flour
1 cup yellow cornmeal
2 teaspoons baking soda
½ teaspoon ground allspice
¼ teaspoon ground ginger
1 teaspoon salt
1¾ cups sour milk or buttermilk
¾ cup molasses
¼ cup light cream or evaporated milk

1 Position the rack in the center of the oven and preheat to 350 degrees F. Lightly grease and flour a 9¼-by-5¼-by-2¾-inch loaf pan.

2 In a large bowl, blend together the two flours, cornmeal, baking soda, allspice, ginger, and salt. In a medium bowl, beat the sour milk, molasses, and cream until smooth. Combine the two mixtures, blending until the dry ingredients are well moistened.

3 Scrape the batter into the prepared pan and bake for 55 to 60 minutes, or until a cake tester or wooden toothpick inserted into the center of the bread comes out clean and the top is golden brown. Remove from the oven and cool the pan on a wire rack for 5 to 10 minutes before removing the loaf from the pan.

# Vermont Johnnycake

MAKES: *1 loaf*

2 cups all-purpose flour
1 cup corn flour
4½ teaspoons baking powder
¾ teaspoon salt
3 large eggs
1 cup milk
¾ cup melted vegetable shortening
½ cup maple syrup

1 Position the rack in the center of the oven and preheat to 400 degrees F. Lightly grease and flour a 9-inch square baking pan.

2 In a large bowl, blend together the two flours, baking powder, and salt. In a medium bowl, beat the eggs until foamy before beating in the milk, shortening, and syrup. Combine the two mixtures, blending until the dry ingredients are well moistened.

3 Scrape the batter into the prepared pan and bake for 35 to 40 minutes, or until a cake tester or wooden toothpick inserted into the center of the bread comes out clean and the top is golden brown. Remove from the oven and cool the pan on a wire rack for 5 to 10 minutes before removing the loaf from the pan.

# Zucchini Bread

MAKES: *1 loaf*

2½ cups all-purpose flour
1 teaspoon baking powder
1 teaspoon baking soda
2 teaspoons ground cinnamon
1 cup finely chopped seedless raisins
½ teaspoon salt
2 large eggs
¾ cup melted margarine or butter
1 teaspoon almond extract
1½ cups warm honey
2 cups grated zucchini

1  Position the rack in the center of the oven and preheat to 350 degrees F. Lightly grease and flour a 9¼-by-5¼-by-2¾-inch loaf pan.

2  In a large bowl, blend together the flour, baking powder, baking soda, cinnamon, raisins, and salt. In a medium bowl, beat the eggs until foamy before beating in the margarine, almond extract, and honey. Stir in the zucchini. Combine the two mixtures, blending until the dry ingredients are well moistened.

3  Scrape the batter into the prepared pan and bake for 55 to 60 minutes, or until a cake tester or wooden toothpick inserted into the center of the bread comes out clean and the top is golden brown. Remove from the oven and cool the pan on a wire rack for 5 to 10 minutes before removing the loaf from the pan.

# ALMOND STREUSEL COFFEE CAKE

MAKES: *6 to 8 servings*

## STREUSEL

½ cup granulated sugar
½ cup firmly packed brown sugar
¼ cup all-purpose flour
4 teaspoons ground cinnamon
¼ cup butter or margarine, at room temperature
1 cup quick-cooking rolled oats
½ cup toasted chopped almonds

## BATTER

¾ cup margarine, at room temperature
1½ cups granulated sugar
3 large eggs
1 cup plain yogurt or sour cream
1½ teaspoons vanilla extract
½ teaspoon almond extract
2½ cups all-purpose flour
2 teaspoons baking powder
1 teaspoon baking soda
1 teaspoon salt

**1**  Position the rack in the center of the oven and preheat to 350 degrees F. Lightly grease and flour the bottom of a 13-by-9-inch baking pan.

**2**  To make the streusel, in a medium bowl, blend together the two sugars, flour, and cinnamon. Using a pastry blender or two knives scissor-fashion, cut in the butter until the mixture resembles coarse crumbs. Stir in the oats and almonds. Set aside.

**3**  To make the batter, in a medium bowl, beat the margarine and sugar until light and fluffy. Beat in the eggs, one at a time, beating vigorously after each addition. Beat in the sour cream, vanilla and almond extract. In a large bowl, blend together the flour, baking powder, baking soda, and salt. Combine the two mixtures, blending until the dry ingredients are moistened.

**4**  Spoon half of the batter into the prepared pan. Sprinkle on half of the streusel mixture over the top of the batter in the pan. Top with the remaining batter and sprinkle with the remaining streusel.

**5**  Bake for 45 to 50 minutes, or until a cake tester or wooden pick inserted into the center of the cake comes out clean. Remove the pan from the oven and cool on a wire rack for 5 to 7 minutes. Serve warm.

SERVING SUGGESTION: **Serve with a bowl of fruit.**

# Black Forest Cherry Coffee Cake

MAKES: *6 to 8 servings*

## FILLING

2 tablespoons packed light-brown sugar
2 tablespoons cornstarch or arrowroot
One 16-ounce can pitted red cherries
1 teaspoon almond extract
6 to 8 drops red food color (optional)
1 cup finely ground almonds (optional)

## BATTER

½ cup all-purpose flour
2 tablespoons Dutch-processed cocoa powder
1 tablespoon packed light-brown sugar
¼ teaspoon baking powder
Pinch of salt
2 tablespoons butter or margarine, at room temperature
⅓ cup evaporated milk or heavy cream
1 teaspoon chocolate or vanilla extract

**1** Position the rack in the center of the oven and preheat to 375 degrees F. Lightly grease and flour the bottom of a 13-by-9-inch baking pan.

**2** To make the filling, combine the brown sugar, cornstarch, and cherries in a saucepan. Place the pan over medium heat and cook, stirring occasionally, until the mixture boils and thickens slightly. Remove from the heat and stir in the almond extract, food color, and almonds. Spoon into the prepared baking pan.

**3** To make the batter, in a large bowl, combine the flour, cocoa powder, brown sugar, baking powder, and salt. Using a pastry blender or two knives scissor-fashion, cut in the butter until the mixture resembles fine meal. Add the milk and chocolate extract and blend until smooth. Spoon the batter over the cherries in the pan.

**4** Bake for 20 to 25 minutes, or until a cake tester or wooden toothpick inserted into the center of the cake comes out clean. Remove the pan from the oven and cool on a wire rack for 5 to 7 minutes. Serve warm or cooled.

# Blackberry–Lemon Coffee Cake

MAKES: *6 to 8 servings*

¾ cup crushed Rice Krispies™ cereal
1½ cups all-purpose flour
¾ cup granulated sugar
½ cup butter or margarine, at room temperature
½ teaspoon baking powder
½ teaspoon baking soda
¼ teaspoon salt
1 large egg
¾ cup buttermilk or sour milk
1 teaspoon grated lemon zest
½ cup blackberry preserves

**1** Position the rack in the center of the oven and preheat to 350 degrees F. Lightly grease a 9-inch square or round baking pan.

**2** In a large bowl, blend together the cereal, flour, and sugar. Using a pastry cutter or two knives scissor-fashion, cut in the margarine until the mixture resembles coarse meal. Reserve ½ cup of this mixture for topping. To the remainder, blend in the baking powder, baking soda, and salt. In a medium bowl, beat the egg until foamy before beating in the buttermilk and lemon zest. Combine the two mixtures, blending until the dry ingredients are moistened.

**3** Spoon two-thirds of the batter into the prepared pan. Gently spread the blackberry preserves over the top. Dot the remaining batter over the top of the preserves. Sprinkle the reserved crumble mix over the top.

**4** Bake for 35 to 40 minutes, or until a cake tester or wooden toothpick inserted near the edge of the cake (not into the preserves) comes out clean. Remove the pan from the oven and cool on a wire rack for 5 to 7 minutes. Serve warm.

# Chocolate Coffee Cake

MAKES: *10 to 12 servings*

½ cup finely ground almonds
2½ cups all-purpose flour
2 teaspoons baking powder
1 teaspoon baking soda
¼ teaspoon salt
½ cup Dutch-processed cocoa powder
1½ cups dried apricots, finely diced
1 cup vegetable shortening
One 8-ounce package cream cheese, at room temperature
2¼ cups granulated sugar
5 large eggs
1½ teaspoons Amaretto liqueur

**1** Position the rack in the center of the oven and preheat to 350 degrees F. Grease and flour a 10-inch Bundt pan. Press ¼ cup of the almonds up the outer sides of the pan.

**2** In a large bowl, blend together the remaining almonds, flour, baking powder, baking soda, salt, cocoa powder, and diced apricots. In a medium bowl, beat shortening, cream cheese, and sugar until smooth. Beat in the eggs one at a time, beating vigorously after each addition. Beat in the Amaretto. Combine the two mixtures, blending until the dry ingredients are just moistened.

**3** Carefully spoon the batter into the prepared baking pan. Bake for 45 to 50 minutes, or until a cake tester or wooden toothpick inserted into the center of the cake comes out clean. Remove the pan from the oven and cool on a wire rack for 5 to 7 minutes before inverting onto a wire rack to cool completely. Serve warm.

# Cinnamon Coffee Cake

MAKES: *8 to 10 servings*

**TOPPING**
½ cup firmly packed brown sugar
½ cup finely chopped walnuts
2 tablespoons all-purpose flour
2 teaspoons ground cinnamon
2 tablespoons canola oil

**BATTER**
1½ cups all-purpose flour
½ cup granulated sugar
2½ teaspoons baking powder
½ teaspoon salt
1 large egg white
¼ cup canola oil
¾ cup milk

**1**  Position the rack in the center of the oven and preheat to 375 degrees F. Lightly grease and flour the bottom of an 8-inch square or round baking pan.

**2**  To make the topping, in a small bowl, combine the brown sugar, walnuts, flour, cinnamon, and oil and mix until crumbly. Set aside.

**3**  To make the batter, in a large bowl, blend together the flour, sugar, baking powder, and salt. In a medium bowl, beat the egg white until foamy before beating in the oil and milk. Combine the two mixtures, blending until the dry ingredients are moistened.

**4**  Spoon half of the batter into the prepared baking pan and top the batter with half of the topping. Spoon the remaining batter into the pan and top with the remaining topping. Bake for 30 to 35 minutes, or until a cake tester or wooden toothpick inserted into the center of the cake comes out clean. Remove the pan from the oven and cool on a wire rack for 5 to 7 minutes. Serve warm or cooled.

# Fat-Free Apple Coffee Cake

Makes: *8 to 10 servings*

1 cup all-purpose flour
1½ teaspoons baking powder
¾ cup granulated sugar
½ teaspoon salt
2 large egg whites
⅓ cup skim milk
⅓ cup Karo® light or dark corn syrup
2 apples, peeled, cored, and halved
2 tablespoons cinnamon sugar for
   sprinkling

**1** Position the rack in the center of the oven and preheat to 350 degrees F. Lightly grease and flour the bottom of a 9-inch square or round baking pan.

**2** In a large bowl, blend together the flour, baking powder, sugar, and salt. In a medium bowl, beat the egg whites stiff but not dry before beating in the milk and corn syrup. Combine the two mixtures, blending until the dry ingredients are moistened. Spoon the batter into the prepared pan, arrange the apples over the top, and sprinkle with cinnamon sugar.

**3** Bake for 45 to 50 minutes, or until a cake tester or wooden toothpick inserted into the center of the cake comes out clean. Remove the pan from the oven and cool on a wire rack for 5 to 7 minutes. Serve warm.

# Imperial Coffee Cake

Makes: *6 to 8 servings*

**TOPPING**

½ cup chopped almonds or pecans
1 cup granulated sugar
1 teaspoon ground cinnamon
1 tablespoon butter or margarine, at
    room temperature

**BATTER**

2 cups all-purpose flour
1 teaspoon baking powder
1 teaspoon baking soda
½ teaspoon ground nutmeg
1 tablespoon grated orange zest
1 cup raisins
1 large egg
1 cup buttermilk or sour milk
⅓ cup melted butter or margarine

**1** Position the rack in the center
of the oven and preheat to 350
degrees F. Lightly grease and
flour the bottom of a 13-by-9-by-
1½-inch baking pan.

**2** To make the topping, in a
small bowl, combine the
almonds, sugar, cinnamon, and
butter and stir until the mixture
is crumbly. Set aside.

**3** To make the batter, in a large
bowl, combine the flour, baking
powder, baking soda, nutmeg,
orange zest, and raisins. In a
small bowl, beat together the
egg, buttermilk, and butter.
Combine the two mixtures,
blending until the dry
ingredients are moistened.

**4** Spoon the batter into the
prepared baking pan and
sprinkle the topping over the
batter. Bake for 30 to 35 minutes,
or until a cake tester or wooden
toothpick inserted into the
center of the cake comes out
clean. Remove the pan from the
oven and cool on a wire rack for
5 to 7 minutes. Serve warm.

# Molasses–Walnut Gingerbread

*Makes: 6 to 8 servings*

3½ cups all-purpose flour
2 teaspoons baking soda
½ teaspoon ground ginger
½ teaspoon ground cinnamon
¼ teaspoon ground cloves
¼ teaspoon salt
1 cup chopped walnuts
½ cup vegetable shortening
1 cup packed dark-brown sugar
½ cup dark molasses
1 cup boiling water
2 large eggs

**1** Position the rack in the center of the oven and preheat to 350 degrees F. Lightly grease and flour the bottom of a 9¼-by-5¼-by-2¾-inch baking pan.

**2** In a large bowl, blend together the flour, baking soda, salt, ginger, cinnamon, cloves, and walnuts. In a medium bowl, beat the shortening and sugar until light and fluffy before beating in the molasses and boiling water.

Add the eggs, one at a time, beating vigorously after each addition. Combine the two mixtures, blending until the dry ingredients are moistened.

**3** Spoon the batter into the prepared pan. Bake for 30 to 35 minutes, or until a cake tester or wooden toothpick inserted into the center of the cake comes out clean. Remove the pan from the oven and cool on a wire rack for 5 to 7 minutes. Serve warm or cooled.

# Pecan–Sour Cream Coffee Cake

Makes: *10 to 12 servings*

## TOPPING
¾ cup firmly packed brown sugar
1 tablespoon all-purpose flour
1 teaspoon ground cinnamon
2 tablespoons butter or margarine, at room temperature
1 cup chopped pecans

## BATTER
½ cup butter or margarine
1 cup granulated sugar
3 large eggs
1 cup sour cream
2 cups all-purpose flour
1 teaspoon baking powder
1 teaspoon baking soda
½ cup raisins
¼ teaspoon salt

**1** Position the rack in the center of the oven and preheat to 350 degrees F. Lightly grease and flour the bottom of a 13-by-9-inch baking pan.

**2** To make the topping, in a small bowl, combine the brown sugar, flour, and cinnamon. Cut in the butter until mixture is crumbly. Set aside.

**3** To make the batter, in a medium bowl, beat the butter and sugar until light and fluffy. Add the eggs, one at a time, beating vigorously after each addition. Add the sour cream. In a large bowl, blend together the flour, the baking powder, baking soda, raisins, and salt. Combine the two mixtures, blending until the dry ingredients are moistened.

**4** Spoon the batter into the prepared pan and sprinkle the topping over the batter. Bake for 28 to 30 minutes, or until a cake tester or wooden toothpick inserted into the center of the cake comes out clean. Remove the pan from the oven and cool on a wire rack for 5 to 7 minutes. Serve warm.

## Bread Crumbs (includes cookie and cracker crumbs)

| | |
|---|---|
| 1 cup fresh bread crumbs | equals 2 ounces or 60 grams |
| 1 slice bread with crust | equals ½ cup bread crumbs, |
| 1 cup dried or toasted bread crumbs | equals 4 ounces or 110 grams |
| 1 pound of bread | equals 14 to 20 slices, or 454 grams |
| 1 cup saltine soda crackers crushed | equals 28 crackers |
| 1 cup graham cracker crumbs | equals 7 to 10 crumbled crackers, 4 ounces or 110 grams |
| 1⅓ cups graham cracker crumbs | equals 16 crumbled crackers, |
| 1 cup vanilla wafer crumbs | equals 30 wafers, 4 ounces, or 110 grams |
| 2 cups vanilla wafer crumbs | equals 8 ounces |
| 1⅔ cups chocolate wafer crumbs | equals 22 wafers |
| 1½ cups gingersnap crumbs | equals 20 snaps |
| 2 cups Zwieback crumbs | equals 24 slices, 6 ounces |

## Dairy Products
(includes cream, milk, sour cream, yogurt, and buttermilk)

### CHEESE

| | |
|---|---|
| 8 ounce package cream cheese | equals 1 cup or 16 tablespoons |
| 3 ounce package cream cheese | equals 6 tablespoons |
| 1 pound cheese | equals 4 cups grated cheese |

### CREAM

| | |
|---|---|
| ½ pint heavy cream | equals 1 cup or 2 cups whipped cream |
| 1 cup whipping cream | equals 2 to 2½ cups whipped cream |

### MILK

| | |
|---|---|
| 1 cup dry skim milk | equals 1 quart skim milk when mixed |
| 1 cup whole milk | equals 8 ounces weight |
| 1 cup heavy cream | equals 8⅜ ounces weight |
| One 6 ounce can evaporated milk | equals ⅔ cup evaporated milk |
| One 14½ ounce can evaporated milk | equals 1⅔ cups evaporated milk |
| One cup sweetened condensed milk | equals 10½ ounces weight |
| One 14 ounce can sweetened condensed milk | equals 1½ cups sweetened condensed milk |
| ⅓ cup evaporated milk | equals ⅓ cup dry milk plus 6 tablespoons water |

### SOUR CREAM

| | |
|---|---|
| One 8 ounce package sour cream | equals 1 cup sour cream |

# Eggs

| | |
|---|---|
| 1 large whole egg | equals 3 tablespoons, 2 ounces, or 60 grams |
| 1 cup large whole eggs | equals approx. 5 eggs |
| 1 large egg yolk | equals 1 generous tablespoon |
| 1 cup large egg yolks | equals approx. 12 egg yolks |
| 1 large egg white | equals 2 tablespoons, 1/8 cup |
| 2 large eggs | equals scant ½ cup, 3 medium eggs, or 180 grams |
| 1 cup large eggs | equals 4 to 5 large eggs |
| 1 cup eggs | equals 5 to 6 medium eggs |
| 1 cup egg yolks | equals 12 to 14 large egg yolks |
| 1 cup egg whites | equals 7 to 10 large egg whites |
| 1 large egg | equals 2 egg yolks in the recipe |
| 1 large fresh egg | equals ½ tablespoon dry plus 2½ tablespoons water |
| 3 large egg whites stiffly beaten | equals 3 cups meringue |

# Fats (includes butter, margarine, and vegetable shortening)

| | |
|---|---|
| ½ ounce butter | equals 1 tablespoon or 1/8 stick |
| 1 ounce butter | equals 2 tablespoons or ¼ stick |
| 2 ounces butter | equals 4 tablespoons or ½ stick |
| 1 pound butter | equals 2 cups, 4 sticks, 32 tablespoons, or 454 grams |
| 1/2 pound | equals 1 cup, 1 stick, 8 tablespoons, or 227 grams |
| 1/4 pound | equals ½ cup, 1 stick, 4 tablespoons, or 113 grams |
| 1 cup butter or margarine | equals ⅞ cup of lard |
| 1 cup hydrogenated fat | equals 6⅔ ounces |
| 2 tablespoons | equals ¼ stick, 2 tablespoons, or 1 ounce |

# Dry Ingredients
(includes arrowroot, baking powder, baking soda, cornmeal, cornstarch, cream of tartar, flour, and salt)

## ARROWROOT

| | |
|---|---|
| 1 teaspoon arrowroot | equals 1 teaspoon all-purpose flour or 1 teaspoon cornstarch |
| 1 tablespoon arrowroot | equals 3 tablespoons all-purpose flour or 2 tablespoons cornstarch |
| 1 tablespoon arrowroot | equals 1 tablespoon all-purpose flour plus 1 teaspoon cornstarch |

## BAKING POWDER & BAKING SODA

| | |
|---|---|
| 2 tablespoons baking powder or soda | equals 1 ounce |
| 1½ teaspoons | equals ¼ ounce |
| 1 tablespoon | equals 0.5 ounce |
| 1 teaspoon | equals 0.17 ounce |

## Dry Ingredients (continued)

### CORNMEAL

| | |
|---|---|
| 1 cup cornmeal | equals 3 to 4 ounces cornmeal |
| 1 cup uncooked cornmeal | equals 4 cups cooked cornmeal |

### CORNSTARCH

| | |
|---|---|
| 1 pound sifted cornstarch | equals 4 cups |
| 1 cup sifted cornstarch | equals 4 ounces |
| 1 ounce sifted cornstarch | equals 4 tablespoons, ¼ cup |
| 1 tablespoon sifted cornstarch | equals 0.29 ounce |
| 1 pound unsifted cornstarch | equals 3½ cups |
| 1 cup unsifted cornstarch | equals 4.5 ounces |
| 1 ounce unsifted cornstarch | equals 3½ tablespoons |
| 1 tablespoon unsifted cornstarch | equals 0.2 ounce |

### CREAM OF TARTAR

| | |
|---|---|
| 4 tablespoons | equals 1 ounce or 30 grams |
| 1 tablespoon | equals ¼ ounces or 7 grams |
| 1 teaspoon | equals 0.08 ounce |

### FLOUR

| | |
|---|---|
| 3 tablespoons all-purpose flour | equals ¼ cup |
| 6 tablespoons all-purpose flour | equals ⅓ cup |
| 9 tablespoons all-purpose flour | equals ½ cup |
| 12 tablespoons all-purpose flour | equals ⅔ cup |
| 15 tablespoons all-purpose flour | equals ¾ cup |
| 18 tablespoons all-purpose flour | equals 1 cup |
| 1 pound all-purpose flour | equals 4 cups |
| 1 cup bleached white all-purpose flour | equals 1 cup unbleached white all-purpose flour |
| 1 cup bleached all-purpose flour | equals 1 cup whole-wheat flour |
| 1 cup bleached all-purpose flour | equals ⅞ cup stone ground whole-wheat flour |
| 1 pound sifted bread flour | equals 4 cups |
| 1 cup sifted bread flour | equals 4 ounces |
| 1 pound unsifted bread flour | equals 3½ cups |
| 1 cup unsifted bread flour | equals 4.75 ounces |
| 1 pound sifted cake flour | equals 4¼ cups |
| 1 cup sifted cake flour | equals 3.75 ounces |
| 1 pound unsifted cake flour | equals 3½ cups |
| 1 cup unsifted cake flour | equals 4.5 ounces |

### SALT

| | |
|---|---|
| 5 teaspoons salt | equals 1 ounce or 30 grams |
| 1 1/4 teaspoons | equals ¼ ounce or 7 grams |
| 1 teaspoon | equals 0.2 ounce |

# Sugars (includes granulated, brown, powdered sugar, and molasses)

## BROWN SUGAR

1 pound firmly packed brown sugar            equals 2½ cups

## GRANULATED

1 pound granulated sugar            equals 2¼ cups
1 cup granulated sugar            equals 7 ounces
1 cup granulated sugar            equals 1 cup packed
                                  brown sugar
1 cup granulated sugar            equals 1¾ cups
                                  confectioners sugar
1 tablespoon granulated sugar            equals 1 tablespoon
                                  maple sugar

## HONEY

1 cup honey            equals 12 ounces

## MOLASSES

11 ounces of molasses            equals 1 cups

## POWDERED

1 pound sifted powdered sugar            equals 4 cups
1 cup sifted powdered sugar            equals 4 ounces
1 pound unsifted powdered sugar            equals 3½ cups
1 cup unsifted powdered sugar            equals 4.5 ounces

## SUBSTITUTE

2 teaspoons sugar            equals 1 packet or ¼
                            teaspoon aspartame
1 tablespoon sugar            equals 1½ packets or ½
                            teaspoon aspartame
¼ cup sugar            equals 6 packets or 1¾
                            teaspoons aspartame
1/3 cup sugar            equals 8 packets or 2½
                            teaspoons aspartame
1/2 cup sugar            equals 12 packets or 3½
                            teaspoons aspartame
1 cup sugar            equals 24 packets or 7¼
                            teaspoons aspartame

# Equivalency Chart

## WEIGHT

| | |
|---|---|
| 1/4 oz. | 07 g |
| 1/2 oz. | 17 g |
| 1 oz. | 28 g |
| 2 oz. | 57 g |
| 5 oz. | 142 g |
| 8 oz. | 227 g |
| 12 oz. | 340 g |
| 16 oz. | 454 g |
| 32 oz. | 907 g |
| 64 oz. | 1.8 kg |

## VOLUME

| | |
|---|---|
| 1/4 tsp. | 1.25 ml |
| 1/2 tsp. | 2.5 ml |
| 1 tsp. | 5 ml |
| 1 tbl. | 15 ml |
| 1/4 cup | 59 ml |
| 1/3 cup | 79 ml |
| 1/2 cup | 119 ml |
| 3/4 cup | 177 ml |
| 1 cup | 237 ml |
| 1 pint (2 cups) | 473 ml |
| 1 quart (4 cups) | 946 ml |
| 1 gallon (4 quarts) | 3.78 litres |

## LENGTH

| | |
|---|---|
| 1/4 in. | 5 mm |
| 1/2 in. | 1 cm |
| 3/4 in. | 2 cm |
| 1 in. | 2.5 cm |
| 2 in. | 5 cm |
| 4 in. | 10 cm |
| 1 foot (12 in.) | 30 cm |

## HEAT

| | | |
|---|---|---|
| very cool | 250-275 F | 130-140 C |
| cool | 300 F | 150 C |
| warm | 325 F | 170 C |
| moderate | 350 F | 180 C |
| moderate hot | 375-400 F | 190-200 C |
| hot | 425 F | 220 C |
| very hot | 450-475 F | 230–250 C |